Baba Vanga: 20th Century Prophet

Andrew Parry

Published by Andrew Parry, 2024.

BABA VANGA: 20TH CENTURY PROPHET

First edition. October 12, 2024.

ISBN: 979-8224626250

Written by Andrew Parry.

Table of Contents

Introduction: The Prophets Who Shaped Our Visions of the Future

Throughout history, humanity has sought insight into the mysteries of the future. From ancient civilizations gazing at the stars to modern-day fascination with mysticism, people have always turned to those who seem to possess a special gift—the ability to see beyond the present. Among these individuals are a select few who have left indelible marks on the world with their prophetic visions. Names like Nostradamus and Edgar Cayce continue to echo through time, captivating believers and sceptics alike. These visionaries, with their cryptic and often alarming predictions, have influenced the way we think about destiny, fate, and the unfolding of world events.

Nostradamus, perhaps the most famous prophet in Western history, is renowned for his enigmatic quatrains, written in the 16th century. His prophecies, collected in *Les Prophéties*, have been interpreted to predict everything from the rise of Napoleon and Adolf Hitler to the 9/11 terrorist attacks. His predictions are cloaked in metaphor, often leading to debates about their accuracy. Some see his writings as vague, open to various interpretations, while others are convinced that he possessed a remarkable ability to foresee the future. Nostradamus' influence is so profound that, centuries after his death, his works continue to inspire books, films, and documentaries, all attempting to decode his timeless messages.

In the 20th century, another seer captured the world's attention with his extraordinary abilities. Edgar Cayce, an American psychic known as the "Sleeping Prophet," would enter a trance-like state and give detailed readings on a range of topics, from medical diagnoses to historical events and even predictions of future calamities. Cayce's fame grew as his health readings helped thousands of people, but it was his prophecies that garnered widespread intrigue. He predicted major events such as the stock market crash of 1929 and World War II. One of his most famous predictions, still awaited by many, is the supposed discovery of the lost continent of Atlantis. Cayce's blend of prophecy, healing, and spiritual guidance has made him one of the most studied psychics in modern history.

However, the search for future knowledge didn't end with these two men. In the latter half of the 20th century, a new figure emerged from an unlikely corner of the world: a blind Bulgarian mystic named Baba Vanga. Born Vangelia Pandeva Gushterova in 1911, she lived most of her life in obscurity, only gaining widespread recognition in the later years of her life and even more so after her death in 1996. Unlike Nostradamus and Cayce, who left behind written or documented accounts of their visions, Baba Vanga's predictions were passed down through oral tradition, recorded by those who came to seek her guidance. What makes Baba Vanga particularly intriguing is her reported accuracy rate—some claim as high as 85%—with predictions that supposedly include major world events such as the September 11 attacks, the Fukushima disaster, and the rise of ISIS.

BLIND FROM A YOUNG age due to a freak accident, Baba Vanga's life was steeped in tragedy and hardship, yet it was this blindness, she claimed, that gave her the ability to "see" into the future. Over the years, thousands of people visited her humble home in Bulgaria, seeking answers about their futures, world events, and even the afterlife. Her predictions, often stark and filled with foreboding, gained the attention of global media, with some even saying that leaders from the Soviet Union sought her counsel. Her visions weren't limited to specific individuals—she made bold claims about the fate of entire nations, the progression of scientific discoveries, and the potential cataclysmic end of the world.

Baba Vanga's most famous prophecies stretch across decades, with chilling accuracy attributed to many of her predictions. She reportedly foretold the sinking of the Russian submarine *Kursk* in 2000, predicted the 2004 Indian

Ocean tsunami, and even claimed the rise of Europe's refugee crisis. But it's her forecasts for the future—those that have yet to come to pass—that continue to stir intrigue and anxiety. According to her, the world will face its greatest trials in the coming years, with 2025 marking the beginning of an apocalyptic cycle that will change life on Earth as we know it.

As we delve into the life and legacy of Baba Vanga, it is essential to remember that, like Nostradamus and Edgar Cayce before her, her prophecies remain a subject of debate. While some believe she had an extraordinary gift, others view her predictions as coincidence or misinterpretation. Yet, despite the skepticism, Baba Vanga has secured her place among the great mystics of history, a figure whose legacy continues to provoke both fear and fascination.

In this book, we will explore the woman behind the predictions, the events she is said to have foreseen, and the broader implications of her visions for the future of humanity. Just as Nostradamus and Cayce have shaped our understanding of prophecy, Baba Vanga's predictions beckon us to contemplate what lies ahead.

The Blind Mystic: Baba Vanga's Early Life

Baba Vanga's journey as one of the most renowned mystics in modern history began in the small village of Strumica, part of the Ottoman Empire at the time of her birth in 1911. Her full name was Vangelia Pandeva Gushterova, though she would come to be known by the affectionate moniker "Baba," meaning grandmother, a title that reflected the deep respect people held for her wisdom and predictions. Her childhood, however, was far from ordinary and filled with hardships that would shape her into the prophetic figure the world came to know.

Baba Vanga's early years were marked by tragedy. She lost her mother when she was still a child, and her father, a soldier who fought in World War I, struggled to raise her and her siblings. Despite their financial difficulties, Vanga led a relatively normal childhood until the age of twelve, when a life-altering event forever changed the course of her destiny.

In 1923, a violent storm hit the region. Baba Vanga, who was playing outside, was caught in the fierce winds, which carried her several miles away from her home. When she was eventually found, she was severely injured, her eyes filled with sand and dust. The damage to her vision was irreversible, and despite numerous attempts to heal her, she gradually became blind. This physical blindness, however, seemed to give rise to an inner sight, as Vanga soon began to display an extraordinary ability to foresee events.

Her family, deeply rooted in rural traditions, believed that her blindness had given her a special gift—a window into the spiritual realm. Vanga herself claimed that during her accident, she had experienced visions of the future and had begun receiving messages from otherworldly sources. Her newfound abilities manifested in small ways at first—she would speak of things that had not yet happened, and soon, those around her began to realize that her predictions were startlingly accurate.

It wasn't long before people from her village and neighboring towns began to seek her advice. Word spread quickly about the young blind girl who could predict the future, heal the sick, and communicate with the dead. Despite her humble surroundings and lack of formal education, Vanga's abilities drew the attention of people far and wide, including politicians, scientists, and even Soviet officials, who came to her for guidance during tumultuous times.

As a teenager, Vanga's reputation grew, and by the 1940s, she had become a well-known figure across Bulgaria and beyond. Yet, despite her growing fame, Baba Vanga remained grounded in her rural roots. She never sought wealth or fame for her abilities, choosing instead to live a modest life. Her prophecies, however, became increasingly complex, dealing with both personal and global events.

Her followers believed that her blindness was a blessing, a divine gift that allowed her to see beyond the physical world and into the spiritual realm. She often described her visions as scenes unfolding before her, as if she were watching a film. Sometimes the images were clear, while at other times they were cryptic and required interpretation. Her most famous predictions would come later, but even in these early years, Baba Vanga's reputation as a mystic was solidified.

The early part of Baba Vanga's life sets the stage for her extraordinary journey into the world of prophecy. Her physical blindness, far from being a limitation, became the very thing that elevated her to prominence. In a world that often sought tangible answers to complex problems, Baba Vanga offered something intangible—a glimpse into the future, a sense of direction in uncertain times. As we continue to explore her life and predictions, it becomes clear that her early experiences played a pivotal role in shaping the mystic she would become, a woman whose sightless eyes saw far beyond the present.

A Gift of Prophecy: How Baba Vanga Foretold the Future

Baba Vanga's gift of prophecy was as enigmatic as it was profound, shrouded in mystery and the unexplained. Her journey from a young blind girl in a rural Bulgarian village to one of the most famous mystics in the modern world is a story of extraordinary visions that would shape her legacy. The nature of her gift seemed to emerge naturally after the traumatic event that left her blind, but those closest to her believed that this was a divine blessing, something bestowed upon her to serve a greater purpose.

Baba Vanga often described her visions as coming in the form of images and sounds that appeared unbidden, filling her mind with scenes of both personal and global events. Unlike the cryptic quatrains of Nostradamus or the trance-like state of Edgar Cayce, Baba Vanga's prophecies were often direct and, at times, surprisingly specific. Those who visited her for counsel would often be given clear predictions about their future—sometimes down to exact dates or descriptions of occurrences that would unfold.

One of the most remarkable aspects of Baba Vanga's prophecies was the wide range of topics she covered. While many mystics focus on spiritual or personal matters, Baba Vanga's predictions extended far beyond the individual. She reportedly foresaw major world events, natural disasters, political changes, and even technological advancements that seemed unimaginable during her lifetime. From the fall of the Soviet Union to the September 11 attacks, her predictions have been analyzed and debated for their accuracy, often long after her death.

Baba Vanga never considered herself special, yet she understood that her gift was rare. She spoke of her visions as if they came from a higher power, describing them as messages from invisible forces. According to her, these forces included spiritual beings who conveyed knowledge of the future and insights into the paths humanity was destined to take. She often claimed that she could not control when or how these visions appeared—they simply manifested themselves as if placed in her mind by divine means.

For many of her followers, Baba Vanga's prophecies seemed to hold a startling accuracy. One of her most famous predictions involved the sinking of the Russian submarine *Kursk* in 2000. Years before the disaster, she had warned that "Kursk will be covered with water, and the whole world will weep over it." At the time, most assumed she was referring to the Russian city of Kursk, but after the submarine disaster, which killed 118 people, her words were seen as eerily prophetic.

Similarly, Baba Vanga is said to have predicted the 2004 Indian Ocean tsunami that devastated parts of Southeast Asia. She reportedly foresaw that a massive wave would engulf the coasts, leading to widespread death and destruction. Although there is no official record of when she made this prediction, many point to this event as evidence of her extraordinary foresight.

HER PROPHECIES DIDN'T just focus on disaster. Baba Vanga made predictions about advancements in science and technology, foretelling the invention of medical treatments that would extend human life and even suggesting that, one day, humanity would be able to communicate with extraterrestrial beings. According to her, contact with otherworldly civilizations was inevitable, and it would transform the course of human history. Though these predictions have yet to come to pass, they have captured the imaginations of her followers, who wait in anticipation for the fulfillment of her visions.

Despite her growing fame, Baba Vanga never sought to commercialize her gift. She continued to live modestly, receiving visitors from around the world who came to seek her wisdom. Among these visitors were political figures, scientists, and even ordinary citizens who had heard of her incredible ability to foretell events. Her sessions were simple—there were no elaborate rituals or ceremonies. Those who came to her would sit quietly as she described what she saw for their future, whether it be personal matters or global events. Many left feeling a mixture of awe and dread, aware that her predictions often carried heavy consequences.

Sceptics, of course, argue that Baba Vanga's prophecies are either coincidences or fabrications. They point out that many of her predictions are vague or could be interpreted in various ways, similar to the writings of other famous seers like Nostradamus. Others suggest that her most specific predictions were only documented after the events occurred, raising questions about their authenticity. Yet, for every skeptic, there are countless believers who insist that Baba Vanga's gift was genuine and that her words continue to hold relevance today.

Perhaps the most intriguing aspect of Baba Vanga's prophecies is that they extended far beyond her lifetime. Before her death in 1996, she made predictions for centuries to come, charting humanity's course until the year 5079, which she claimed would mark the end of the world. Her long-range visions included everything from climate disasters to political upheaval, technological breakthroughs, and even human contact with extraterrestrial beings. While some of her predictions have yet to materialize, her timeline remains a topic of fascination and debate, keeping her legacy alive well into the 21st century.

In this chapter, we begin to uncover the extraordinary ability that made Baba Vanga so renowned. Whether her gift was divine, spiritual, or purely a result of circumstance, her prophetic insights have left a profound mark on the world. From the sinking of the *Kursk* to visions of the far-flung future, Baba Vanga's predictions continue to captivate those seeking answers in an uncertain world.

Visions Beyond Sight: The Origins of Baba Vanga's Mysticism

Baba Vanga's mysticism was deeply intertwined with her extraordinary life story, a journey that took her from an ordinary child in rural Bulgaria to a revered prophetess who could seemingly peer into the future. But where did her mystical abilities come from? How did a young girl, left blind by a tragic accident, come to be regarded as one of the most accurate and powerful mystics of the 20th century?

The origins of Baba Vanga's mysticism are often traced back to the traumatic event that left her blind at the age of twelve. The violent storm that swept her away and caused her injury was seen by many as a pivotal moment in her life, not only because it took her sight but because it appeared to awaken a new sense within her. In the years following the accident, Vanga began to experience vivid visions, and she claimed to hear voices that would provide her with information beyond the grasp of ordinary human perception. This transformation, from sighted child to blind mystic, would set the foundation for her life as a seer.

The cultural and spiritual context in which Baba Vanga grew up also played a significant role in shaping her mysticism. Bulgaria, at the time of her birth, was a land rich in folk traditions, many of which were rooted in mysticism, magic, and the supernatural. The Balkan region has a long history of belief in fortune-tellers, spiritual healers, and prophets, and this cultural backdrop created an environment where Baba Vanga's abilities could thrive. People in her village and surrounding areas were more inclined to accept and even revere individuals with extraordinary gifts, seeing them as conduits for divine or spiritual powers.

As Vanga's reputation began to grow, so too did the stories of her mystical abilities. Villagers spoke of how she could predict the future, find lost objects, and heal the sick, all while never leaving her small home. She seemed to possess an uncanny knowledge of events, both personal and global, that she could not have possibly known through conventional means. It was this combination of personal foresight and an inexplicable connection to the larger world that cemented her status as a mystic.

One of the fascinating aspects of Baba Vanga's mysticism was her claim that her visions were not something she sought out, but rather something that happened to her. She often described her experiences as involuntary—images and messages would simply come to her, often without warning. These visions were not vague or abstract, as is often the case with mystics, but clear and vivid, like snapshots of the future playing out in her mind. She claimed to see entire scenes unfold, much like watching a film, and she believed these visions were sent to her by higher powers or spiritual beings.

The spiritual forces Baba Vanga spoke of were central to her understanding of her gift. She described them as invisible entities that existed beyond the physical realm, guiding her visions and imparting knowledge about the future. According to Vanga, these beings were not gods in the traditional sense but rather intermediaries between the divine and the earthly. She saw herself as a vessel through which these spiritual forces could communicate with humanity, offering guidance, warnings, and insights.

Her deep connection to the spiritual world was also reflected in her healing abilities. Many people who visited Baba Vanga were not only seeking predictions about the future but also relief from physical and emotional ailments. She would often prescribe herbal remedies or give advice on how to overcome illness, claiming that her knowledge came directly from her spiritual guides. Some of her followers believed that she had the ability to channel healing energy, and there were countless stories of people being cured after visiting her.

Baba Vanga's mysticism wasn't limited to her personal abilities; it also extended to her understanding of the broader world and humanity's place within it. She often spoke of an interconnectedness between all living things, the past, present, and future, as if everything existed on a continuum that she could access at will. Her prophecies were rooted in this belief that time was not linear but fluid, allowing her to see the events of tomorrow as clearly as the events of today. For Vanga, the future was not set in stone, but a dynamic landscape shaped by human actions, divine will, and the interplay of unseen forces.

As her fame grew, so did the myths surrounding her origins. Some believed that her blindness granted her a supernatural "inner vision," allowing her to see into realms that others could not perceive. Others saw her accident as a symbolic transformation, marking her transition from an ordinary child to a spiritual figure chosen by the divine. Whether these stories were true or embellished, they added to the mystique that surrounded Baba Vanga and her abilities.

Despite the growing number of people who sought her counsel, Baba Vanga remained humble and grounded. She often spoke of her abilities as a burden, not a blessing. The constant flow of visitors, the demands on her time and energy, and the weight of the predictions she made took a toll on her. Yet, she continued to offer her insights, feeling a sense of duty to those who sought her help. In her later years, she expressed concern about the way her gift was being perceived, worrying that people were too focused on the sensational aspects of her prophecies rather than the deeper spiritual truths they conveyed.

The origins of Baba Vanga's mysticism are a fascinating blend of personal tragedy, cultural tradition, and spiritual awakening. From the storm that left her blind to the spiritual forces that guided her visions, Vanga's life was shaped by forces beyond the ordinary. Her mysticism, rooted in the belief that she was a conduit for higher powers, would come to define her legacy as one of the most enigmatic and powerful mystics of the 20th century. Through her visions, she offered the world a glimpse of the unknown, inviting both wonder and fear at the possibilities that lay ahead.

The Legacy of Vangelia: Baba Vanga's Influence on Modern Mysticism

Baba Vanga's remarkable legacy stretches far beyond her life and the modest Bulgarian village where she resided. After her death in 1996, Vanga's influence only continued to grow, establishing her as a towering figure in the realm of modern mysticism. With thousands of prophecies to her name, her followers believe that she was not just a mystic but a bridge between the physical world and the spiritual realms, her predictions leaving a lasting impact on both popular culture and spiritual thought.

Baba Vanga's rise to prominence in the 20th century came during a time when belief in mystical powers was often met with skepticism, particularly in the post-World War II era. Yet, in the shadow of political uncertainty and social upheaval, people continued to turn to mystics like her for guidance and understanding. While her influence was primarily rooted in Eastern Europe, her fame would eventually transcend borders. Her reputation as a mystic who predicted world events made her a household name, especially among those who believed that certain individuals possessed the rare ability to communicate with unseen forces.

One of the key reasons Baba Vanga's legacy has endured is the remarkable accuracy attributed to some of her predictions. Over the years, numerous events have been linked to her prophecies—some of which seemed almost impossible to foresee. For example, her supposed prediction of the September 11 attacks on the World Trade Center in 2001 captured global attention. She is said to have described "two steel birds" that would strike America, a vision interpreted as a reference to the planes that crashed into the towers. While sceptics question the interpretation and timing of such prophecies, her followers remain convinced of her extraordinary foresight.

Her influence on modern mysticism is also closely tied to her ability to foresee technological and scientific advancements. Vanga reportedly predicted many developments that seemed far beyond the scope of her time, including advancements in medicine, such as treatments that would prolong human life. She spoke of humanity's future in space, predicting that by 2028, humans would begin exploring Venus to search for alternative energy sources. Although such predictions have yet to materialize, they point to the wide scope of her vision, which ranged from personal fates to global and cosmic events.

Baba Vanga's mysticism was also revolutionary in that it merged elements of traditional prophecy with more modern concerns. Many of her predictions were focused on the rise and fall of political regimes, global conflicts, and environmental disasters. In this way, her prophecies reflected the anxieties of the 20th and 21st centuries, addressing issues like climate change, economic collapse, and technological warfare. Her followers often point to her foresight of environmental catastrophes, such as the melting of the polar ice caps, which she claimed would occur in the 21st century, drastically altering the world's coastlines. Predictions like these have only deepened the belief that Baba Vanga's visions were rooted in a profound understanding of the trajectory of human history.

IN THE REALM OF MYSTICISM, Vanga's prophecies also introduced a new kind of global perspective. While many mystics focused on localized events or individual fortunes, Baba Vanga's predictions spanned continents and eras, from the collapse of the Soviet Union to the rise of radical political movements in the West. This global scope has cemented her influence, positioning her as not just a regional figure but a mystic whose insights have reverberated across the world.

However, it wasn't just the predictions themselves that defined Baba Vanga's legacy; it was the way she engaged with the spiritual world. Her prophecies were not vague or abstract but often startlingly direct. While she spoke of great calamities and political upheavals, she also gave personal guidance to those who came to her seeking advice. This combination of personal and global insight gave her a unique place among modern mystics. She became not only a seer of world events but a personal oracle for those in need of spiritual direction.

Baba Vanga's legacy also lives on in the way her life has inspired future generations of mystics, seers, and spiritual healers. Many of those who followed in her footsteps saw her as a figure who transcended the limitations of human perception. Her blindness, far from being a disadvantage, was viewed as a gift that allowed her to see into realms beyond the physical world. This narrative of overcoming physical limitations to access spiritual truth has inspired countless other mystics who see Vanga as a role model in their own spiritual journeys.

The mysticism associated with Baba Vanga has had a profound influence on how people perceive prophecy and divination in the modern world. Her predictions are often cited in discussions of supernatural phenomena, alongside the works of other famous seers like Nostradamus and Edgar Cayce. Popular media continues to reference her prophecies, especially when major global events align with her predictions. Documentaries, books, and television programs have examined her life, attempting to decode the secrets behind her prophecies. While sceptics often challenge the accuracy and legitimacy of her predictions, her influence in shaping modern mysticism is undeniable. Additionally, Baba Vanga's fame was not just confined to the spiritual domain—her legacy has extended into popular culture as well. Stories of her life and predictions have appeared in everything from news reports to films, where she is often portrayed as a symbol of humanity's fascination with the unknown. Her name has become synonymous with prophecy, and many who hear of her visions are struck by the mystery and intrigue surrounding her life.

Her continued relevance in the public imagination speaks to a broader human desire for understanding and control over the future. In times of uncertainty, mystics like Baba Vanga offer not just predictions but a sense of connection to something greater than ourselves—whether it be a divine force, a spiritual realm, or simply a deeper intuition about the course of events. Baba Vanga's life and work have left a mark that transcends time, offering both comfort and caution to those who seek answers in an unpredictable world. In the grand tapestry of mysticism, Baba Vanga occupies a unique space. Her life, her predictions, and her extraordinary abilities have influenced the way people think about prophecy and the spiritual realm. Though she passed away in 1996, her legacy continues to inspire and captivate, her prophecies stretching far into the future, long after her lifetime. Whether seen as a true visionary or a subject of legend, Baba Vanga's influence on modern mysticism remains profound and enduring.

A Woman of the People: Baba Vanga's Rise to Fame

Baba Vanga's journey from a small village in Bulgaria to becoming one of the most famous mystics of the 20th century is a story of profound humility and unexpected fame. Despite her extraordinary abilities and global reputation, she remained deeply rooted in the simple life she had always known. Baba Vanga's rise to fame was not the result of self-promotion or ambition, but rather a natural progression as word of her abilities spread far and wide. She was, above all else, a woman of the people—accessible, humble, and devoted to those who sought her help.

In the early years, Baba Vanga's abilities were known primarily within her village of Rupite and the surrounding areas. Villagers would come to her with everyday problems, seeking guidance on matters of health, lost items, or relationships. Her reputation as a healer and seer grew steadily as more and more people came away from their visits with stories of her startling accuracy and kindness. She never turned anyone away, and it was this open-door policy that endeared her to the local community.

At the heart of her rise to fame was her profound connection to the common people. Unlike many mystics or spiritual figures who isolate themselves from the public or surround themselves with an air of exclusivity, Baba Vanga remained deeply accessible. She lived in a modest home, dressed simply, and carried out her daily tasks just like any other villager. She did not charge for her services, and the financial support she received from those who visited her was modest. It was this simplicity and her unwillingness to seek personal wealth or fame that made her all the more respected. In the eyes of her followers, Baba Vanga was a beacon of wisdom, not a figure of grandeur.

As her fame began to spread, it wasn't long before more prominent figures took notice. By the mid-20th century, she was attracting attention from political leaders, intellectuals, and even scientists. In the post-war period, when Bulgaria was under Communist rule, Baba Vanga's fame became even more widespread, reaching into the highest levels of government. It's said that even Soviet leaders sought her advice on political matters and national affairs. Despite the political tensions of the time, Baba Vanga's abilities transcended the ideological divide. Her counsel was seen not as a matter of politics but as something more profound—a spiritual insight into the human condition and the events that shaped the world.

However, Baba Vanga's rise to fame wasn't without its challenges. As her reputation grew, so did the skepticism surrounding her abilities. Some viewed her as a fraud or a charlatan, while others criticized the attention she received from high-profile individuals. Nevertheless, these criticisms never seemed to affect Baba Vanga herself. She remained steadfast in her beliefs and continued to live a life of simplicity, focusing on helping those who came to her. Her fame did not change her character; it simply magnified the reach of her influence.

ONE OF THE MOST REMARKABLE aspects of Baba Vanga's rise to fame was how it extended beyond Bulgaria. By the 1970s and 1980s, her reputation had crossed borders, attracting people from across Europe and even beyond. Journalists, filmmakers, and researchers visited her, hoping to understand the source of her prophecies and the secret to her accuracy. She became the subject of numerous documentaries and interviews, and her predictions were reported in newspapers and magazines worldwide. Despite this international attention, she continued to live in her small home in Rupite, unbothered by the growing interest in her abilities.

Her appeal lay not only in the accuracy of her predictions but also in her humility and the personal connections she made with those who visited her. Baba Vanga did not seek to distance herself from the people who came to her for help. She treated everyone equally, whether they were a politician, a scientist, or a simple villager. Her fame did not diminish her warmth, and those who met her often spoke of her kindness and compassion.

At the core of Baba Vanga's rise to fame was her gift for prophecy, but it was her genuine connection to people that truly cemented her legacy. She saw herself not as a mystic on a pedestal but as a servant of those in need. Whether foreseeing global events or providing comfort to someone struggling with personal difficulties, Baba Vanga approached every person and situation with the same dedication. She became a symbol of hope in a world filled with uncertainty, a mystic who belonged to the people rather than the elite.

As her influence grew, the scope of her predictions expanded. She began to offer visions not only of personal fates but of global events—political upheavals, natural disasters, and technological advancements. These predictions brought even more attention, further fueling her fame. People began traveling great distances to seek her guidance, convinced that her insights held the key to understanding their futures and the fate of the world.

Despite her growing fame, Baba Vanga remained grounded. She never sought to commercialize her abilities or exploit her fame for personal gain. Instead, she continued to live simply, seeing herself as a vessel for the divine messages she received. Her prophecies, whether personal or global, were delivered with the same calm demeanor, and she never claimed to be infallible or omniscient. She was, above all, a humble woman who believed in the gift she had been given and the responsibility it carried.

As we look back on Baba Vanga's rise to fame, it is clear that her impact was not only due to the accuracy of her predictions but also her unwavering connection to the people she served. She became famous not because she sought the limelight, but because her abilities and compassion spoke for themselves. To the world, she was a mystic; to those who knew her, she was a humble woman with an extraordinary gift—a woman of the people, who rose to fame by remaining true to herself.

The Chilling Prediction of 2025: The Start of the Apocalypse?

Among Baba Vanga's many prophecies, none is as unsettling as her prediction for the year 2025. This year, she claimed, would mark the beginning of a global apocalypse, a cataclysmic chain of events that would drastically alter life as we know it. Unlike her more cryptic predictions, the prophecy for 2025 is chillingly direct, warning of a devastating conflict in Europe that would impact the population on an unprecedented scale. The world would not end in an instant, but the events triggered in 2025 would set humanity on a path toward a slow and painful decline—culminating centuries later in the ultimate destruction of Earth.

The idea that 2025 would be the start of a long-drawn-out apocalypse is deeply unsettling for many, particularly as global tensions rise and the political landscape remains uncertain. Baba Vanga's prediction comes at a time when the world is already grappling with various crises—climate change, geopolitical instability, pandemics, and resource shortages. To her followers, the alignment of these events with her forecast adds a layer of ominous significance to her prophecy.

According to reports, Baba Vanga saw a conflict erupting in Europe in 2025, one that would devastate the continent's population. The nature of this conflict remains vague, as she did not specify whether it would be a war, a series of natural disasters, or perhaps a combination of both. Some speculate that she may have been referring to political or military strife, while others believe her prophecy could be linked to environmental collapse or even a global economic disaster. Whatever the cause, the result, she claimed, would be catastrophic for Europe and would send shockwaves throughout the rest of the world.

What makes this prediction particularly eerie is that it mirrors the fears and anxieties many people already feel about the future. With rising tensions between global powers, the threat of military conflict in Europe is not far-fetched. The war in Ukraine, for example, has reignited concerns about stability in the region and the potential for a broader conflict to erupt. The idea of an apocalyptic event stemming from this part of the world feels all too plausible, and Baba Vanga's prophecy seems to tap into the collective unease about the precarious state of international relations.

But Baba Vanga's prediction for 2025 is not just about war or conflict. It speaks to a broader collapse of systems—political, economic, and social—that will destabilize the world. She described the events of 2025 as the beginning of the end, with humanity slowly unraveling over the coming centuries. This vision is both terrifying and strangely compelling. Unlike traditional apocalyptic scenarios that involve sudden destruction, Baba Vanga's vision of the future unfolds over a much longer timeline, with the world gradually succumbing to chaos, conflict, and environmental decay.

According to her timeline, humanity's ultimate demise wouldn't occur until 5079. However, the years between 2025 and that distant future would be filled with crises that would push human civilization to the brink. In 2028, she predicted that humans would begin exploring Venus in search of alternative energy sources, a sign of our desperation as resources on Earth begin to dwindle.

By 2033, she claimed, the polar ice caps would melt, drastically raising sea levels and submerging entire coastal regions. Each of these events, she said, would add to the strain on human society, leading to further instability and conflict.

The most unsettling aspect of Baba Vanga's prophecy is the idea that the world will not end quickly but will instead suffer a slow, agonizing collapse. Her followers interpret this as a warning that the decisions humanity makes now will determine how rapidly we descend into chaos. Her vision of 2025, while ominous, also serves as a potential call to action—a reminder that our actions today have consequences for the future, and that the only way to avoid total destruction is to make meaningful changes before it's too late.

Of course, sceptics are quick to point out that Baba Vanga's prophecies are often vague and open to interpretation. They argue that her prediction of a European conflict in 2025 could be a reflection of the ongoing political tensions in the region, rather than a specific foretelling of a new apocalyptic event. After all, conflict in Europe has been a recurring theme throughout history, and predicting unrest in the region is not necessarily ground-breaking. Similarly, her warnings about environmental disaster and resource depletion echo concerns that scientists and environmentalists have been raising for decades.

However, even sceptics cannot deny the eerie accuracy of some of Baba Vanga's past predictions. She reportedly foresaw the September 11 attacks, the 2004 Indian Ocean tsunami, and the Fukushima nuclear disaster, all of which were global events that reshaped the world in profound ways. The fact that some of her previous prophecies have come to pass adds weight to her prediction for 2025, leaving many to wonder whether we are truly on the verge of something catastrophic.

As the world edges closer to 2025, the tension surrounding Baba Vanga's prophecy continues to grow. Some see it as a warning that we should not ignore, while others view it as a reflection of the uncertainties that have always defined human history. Either way, the idea that we could be on the brink of a major global shift is unsettling. If Baba Vanga's vision holds any truth, then 2025 may be a turning point for humanity, marking the beginning of an era of upheaval that will reshape the world for generations to come.

While her prediction paints a grim picture of the future, it also offers a glimpse into the potential for survival. Baba Vanga often spoke of humanity's resilience and adaptability, even in the face of disaster. Though her vision of the future is dark, it suggests that humanity will not be wiped out immediately. Instead, we will endure, adapt, and find ways to navigate the challenges ahead—albeit through a drawn-out and difficult process.

As we approach 2025, it is clear that Baba Vanga's chilling prediction has already left its mark. Whether it proves to be accurate or not, her vision has sparked conversations about the fragility of our world and the importance of preparing for the future. In many ways, the prophecy serves as a reflection of our own fears about the coming decades, and as a reminder that while the future is uncertain, it is also something we have the power to shape.

Prophecies of War: Europe's Dark Future

Among the many predictions made by Baba Vanga, her foretelling of war and conflict in Europe stands out as one of the most ominous and troubling. Throughout her life, the blind mystic spoke frequently of dark times ahead for the continent, warning that Europe would face immense challenges that could lead to devastating consequences for its population. Her prophecies of war have become especially relevant in recent times, with growing political instability, economic uncertainty, and rising tensions between global powers. In this chapter, we will explore Baba Vanga's prophecies of war in Europe, their potential implications, and the dark future she envisioned for the continent.

According to Baba Vanga, Europe's future would be shaped by conflict—conflict that would not only affect the nations involved but reverberate across the entire world. While some of her prophecies were specific, others were more symbolic or cryptic, leaving much to interpretation. One of her most chilling predictions was that Europe would be devastated by a great war that would lead to a massive loss of life, widespread destruction, and an irreversible shift in the global balance of power.

Baba Vanga's prophecy for 2025 predicted that a conflict would erupt in Europe that would have far-reaching consequences. She claimed that this conflict would devastate the population, leading to suffering on a scale not seen since the world wars of the 20th century. Although she did not specify the exact nature of the conflict, her followers believe that it could involve a combination of political, military, and environmental factors. In an era marked by rising nationalism, geopolitical struggles, and increasing climate-related disasters, the idea of a conflict that could engulf Europe does not seem far-fetched.

Some interpretations of Baba Vanga's prophecies suggest that the conflict she foresaw may not be a traditional war but rather a combination of crises—economic collapse, refugee crises, and environmental disasters—that would spark unrest and violence across the continent. In her visions, she described a Europe that was fractured and divided, with nations turning against one another and struggling to maintain stability. This division would lead to widespread chaos, with populations displaced, economies crumbling, and governments unable to maintain order.

One of the more alarming aspects of Baba Vanga's prophecy is that the conflict in Europe would not remain isolated to the continent. Instead, it would have ripple effects across the globe, potentially drawing in other world powers and creating a situation that could spiral out of control. This notion of Europe being a flashpoint for a larger global conflict is particularly resonant in today's world, where tensions between NATO, Russia, and other major powers are at a precarious point. Baba Vanga's prophecy suggests that Europe could be the site of a new type of war—one that may involve conventional military forces but could also include cyber warfare, economic warfare, or even conflicts over resources and migration.

A KEY THEME IN BABA Vanga's prophecies of war is the idea of Europe being weakened and divided. She predicted that many European countries would face internal struggles, with political polarization and economic disparity driving a wedge between the populations. These divisions, she claimed, would make the continent vulnerable to external threats, leading to a breakdown in alliances and partnerships that had once maintained peace and stability. The fracturing of Europe, in her vision, would leave it defenseless against larger powers seeking to exploit the chaos.

Her followers have often pointed to the rise of far-right political movements, the ongoing refugee crisis, and the economic instability caused by events like Brexit as evidence that Baba Vanga's prophecy of a divided Europe is already beginning to come true. In this sense, her predictions are seen as a warning that unless these issues are addressed, the continent could be headed toward a dark and uncertain future, one marked by war and destruction. In addition to political and military conflicts, Baba Vanga also spoke of environmental disasters that would exacerbate the situation in Europe. She predicted that climate change would play a significant role in destabilizing the continent, with natural disasters such as floods, droughts, and extreme weather events further straining already fragile political systems. In her vision, these environmental crises would create a perfect storm of conditions that could lead to widespread conflict, as nations scramble for resources and populations are displaced by rising sea levels and food shortages.

Baba Vanga's prophecies also suggested that Europe would be at the center of a larger global conflict involving not just traditional powers like the United States and Russia but also new emerging powers from Asia and the Middle East. She envisioned a world where the old geopolitical order would be upended, with alliances shifting and new powers rising to challenge the dominance of Europe and the West. This realignment of global power could lead to new forms of conflict, both in Europe and beyond. While some may dismiss Baba Vanga's prophecies as exaggerated or overly dramatic, there is no denying that the world is currently facing a period of intense uncertainty. The possibility of conflict in Europe, whether due to political, economic, or environmental factors, is a very real concern. As the continent grapples with a range of issues, from the ongoing war in Ukraine to the effects of climate change, the idea of a future marked by division and conflict does not seem as distant as it once might have.

Despite the dark picture painted by her predictions, Baba Vanga's prophecies also contain a message of resilience. She believed that while Europe would face great challenges, humanity would ultimately find ways to adapt and survive. However, her vision suggests that this survival will come at a great cost, with the world transformed by the events that unfold in Europe. The Europe of the future, according to her, will not be the Europe we know today. It will be a continent reshaped by war, division, and struggle, but one that may still offer hope for those who can navigate the difficult path ahead. As we look toward the future, Baba Vanga's prophecies of war in Europe serve as a stark reminder of the fragility of peace. Whether her vision for 2025 proves to be accurate or not, the warning signs are already visible. Europe, once a beacon of stability and cooperation, is facing a period of immense challenge. Whether it can avoid the fate foretold by Baba Vanga depends not only on the actions of its leaders but on the ability of its people to unite in the face of adversity. The future remains uncertain, but Baba Vanga's prophecies offer a glimpse into what could be—a dark future for Europe if the right course is not set today.

Venus Exploration: A Search for Energy in 2028

A mong Baba Vanga's many bold predictions, one that stands out as particularly futuristic and intriguing is her prophecy regarding the exploration of Venus in the year 2028. She claimed that humanity, in its desperate search for new energy sources, would begin exploring Venus as a potential solution to Earth's growing energy crisis. This prediction, while seemingly far-fetched given the planet's inhospitable conditions, taps into our ongoing quest for alternative energy and the lengths to which humanity might go to secure its survival.

As Earth's population grows and our dependence on fossil fuels continues, the search for alternative energy sources has become one of the most critical issues of our time. Baba Vanga's prediction aligns with these concerns, envisioning a future where Earth's resources are so depleted that humanity looks beyond its own planet to find sustainable energy. While Venus may seem like an unlikely candidate for such exploration, the underlying message in her prophecy reflects a larger, more urgent issue: the depletion of Earth's resources and the necessity of finding new solutions.

Venus, the second planet from the Sun, has long captured the imagination of scientists and science fiction enthusiasts alike. Its proximity to Earth makes it a tempting target for exploration, but its extreme conditions—surface temperatures that can melt lead, an atmosphere thick with carbon dioxide, and clouds of sulfuric acid—pose significant challenges. Despite these conditions, Baba Vanga's prediction suggests that humanity will find a way to overcome these obstacles in its search for energy, driven by necessity as Earth's own resources dwindle.

In recent years, the concept of space exploration as a solution to Earth's resource shortages has gained traction, particularly with the growing interest in colonizing Mars and mining asteroids for minerals. Baba Vanga's prophecy of exploring Venus for energy may not be so far removed from these real-world discussions. As technological advancements continue to push the boundaries of space exploration, the idea of tapping into the resources of other planets becomes increasingly plausible. While Venus is currently seen as one of the least hospitable planets in the solar system, future advancements in technology and energy production could make such an endeavor possible.

The year 2028, as predicted by Baba Vanga, may seem distant, but in the context of space exploration, it is just around the corner. Current plans for space exploration are already being developed, with NASA, private companies like SpaceX, and other international space agencies working toward missions that aim to explore Mars, the Moon, and even more distant celestial bodies. The prediction that Venus could be the focus of such missions aligns with the growing interest in harnessing space for the future survival of humanity.

BABA VANGA'S PROPHECY of Venus exploration can be interpreted in several ways. On one level, it may represent humanity's increasing desperation to find alternative energy solutions. As climate change accelerates, natural resources become scarcer, and global populations rise, the need for sustainable and renewable energy sources becomes more pressing. In this light, her prediction may not be a literal forecast of Venus exploration but rather a symbolic warning about the lengths to which humanity may go to address its energy crisis.

On another level, her prophecy could be seen as a vision of scientific and technological breakthroughs that allow humanity to explore planets like Venus, despite their extreme conditions. If technology advances far enough, what seems impossible today—harnessing energy from Venus—could become a reality. Baba Vanga's foresight may be pointing to a future where humanity not only solves its energy crisis but also expands its reach into the solar system, using resources from other planets to sustain life on Earth.

Interestingly, her prediction also raises questions about the ethics of space exploration and the exploitation of other celestial bodies for human gain. Just as humanity has depleted many of Earth's natural resources, the idea of mining or extracting energy from other planets brings with it ethical considerations. Will humanity repeat the same mistakes in space, exploiting new worlds without considering the long-term consequences? Baba Vanga's prophecy, while futuristic, may also be a cautionary tale about the dangers of unchecked resource extraction, whether on Earth or beyond.

The notion of Venus exploration for energy also brings to mind the many challenges humanity would face in attempting such a feat. Venus's surface is one of the most hostile environments in the solar system, with temperatures reaching over 450 degrees Celsius (850 degrees Fahrenheit), atmospheric pressure 90 times that of Earth, and corrosive clouds of sulfuric acid. However, recent discoveries in Venus's atmosphere have reignited interest in the planet. In 2020, scientists detected traces of phosphine gas in the planet's clouds, a potential indicator of microbial life. This discovery has led to renewed discussions about Venus's potential as a site for scientific exploration, and possibly, as Baba Vanga predicted, for future energy solutions.

If humanity were to explore Venus in 2028, as Baba Vanga foretold, it would likely require breakthroughs in energy technology, space travel, and environmental protection. New forms of energy generation, such as fusion power or advanced solar technologies, might be necessary to survive Venus's harsh conditions. Additionally, space travel would need to advance significantly to transport humans or machines to Venus, sustain life or operations there, and return with the harvested energy. These challenges, while immense, are not insurmountable. If anything, Baba Vanga's prediction encourages us to push the boundaries of what we think is possible in the realm of space exploration.

In her prophecy, the exploration of Venus is not just a scientific endeavor; it is a reflection of humanity's resilience and resourcefulness in the face of existential challenges. As Earth's resources become increasingly scarce, humanity must look to new frontiers to ensure its survival. Baba Vanga's vision of exploring Venus for energy is a testament to the enduring human spirit—the drive to seek out new solutions, even in the most unlikely of places.

While it remains to be seen whether Baba Vanga's prediction of Venus exploration in 2028 will come true, the underlying message of her prophecy is clear. Humanity is at a crossroads, and the decisions we make today about energy, technology, and exploration will shape our future. Whether we turn to Venus, Mars, or another celestial body for solutions, the quest for energy will continue to define the next chapter of human history.

As the clock ticks toward 2028, Baba Vanga's prediction offers both a glimpse of hope and a challenge. The idea of exploring Venus for energy may seem fantastical now, but in an era of rapid technological advancement and growing global crises, it serves as a reminder that the future is full of possibilities—both wondrous and daunting.

Melting Ice Caps: Baba Vanga's Climate Warnings for 2033

Among Baba Vanga's prophecies, her prediction regarding the melting of the polar ice caps in 2033 stands out as both a stark warning and a reflection of the growing concern over climate change. She foresaw that this event would trigger a dramatic rise in global sea levels, leading to widespread devastation along the world's coastlines. This prophecy aligns closely with contemporary scientific forecasts about the effects of global warming, adding weight to her vision of a future in which climate change plays a central role in reshaping life on Earth.

Baba Vanga's prediction for 2033 fits within a broader narrative of environmental collapse. She warned that as the polar ice caps melted, sea levels would rise to catastrophic levels, submerging entire regions and displacing millions of people. In her vision, the world would face massive flooding, particularly in low-lying coastal areas, leading to a global humanitarian crisis. The loss of habitable land, combined with the economic and social upheavals that such a disaster would cause, would push humanity to the brink.

The year 2033 may seem distant, but for those studying climate change, the timeline is alarmingly plausible. Scientists have long warned that the continued rise in global temperatures, driven by greenhouse gas emissions, is accelerating the melting of the polar ice caps. The Arctic, in particular, is warming at twice the rate of the rest of the planet, and the ice sheets in both Greenland and Antarctica are losing mass at an unprecedented rate. According to current projections, sea levels could rise by several feet by the end of the century, but Baba Vanga's prophecy suggests that this process could unfold even faster, with devastating consequences.

Baba Vanga's prediction of melting ice caps is not just about rising seas—it reflects the broader, interconnected impacts of climate change on the global ecosystem. She spoke of natural disasters, food shortages, and mass migrations as direct results of the environmental crises triggered by the melting ice. The floodwaters, she predicted, would not only submerge cities but also disrupt agriculture, leading to famine and economic instability. In her vision, the melting ice caps were just the beginning of a larger chain reaction of environmental collapse that would push humanity into an era of struggle and survival.

In recent years, the reality of climate change has become impossible to ignore. Record-breaking heatwaves, wildfires, hurricanes, and flooding have all become more frequent and severe, underscoring the urgency of addressing the issue. Baba Vanga's prophecy for 2033 echoes the warnings of climate scientists, who have long predicted that if global temperatures continue to rise unchecked, we will reach a tipping point where the effects of climate change become irreversible. The melting of the polar ice caps is one such tipping point—once the ice is gone, it cannot be restored, and the damage to ecosystems, economies, and human lives will be profound.

FOR BABA VANGA'S FOLLOWERS, her prophecy serves as a reminder that the consequences of inaction are dire. While some of her predictions are open to interpretation, the threat posed by climate change is not. The idea that rising seas could displace millions of people and disrupt global food supplies is no longer a distant possibility—it is a reality that many scientists believe could happen within our lifetimes. Baba Vanga's vision of the future aligns with these scientific forecasts, offering a grim glimpse into the environmental and humanitarian crises that could emerge in the coming decades.

In Baba Vanga's vision, the melting of the ice caps would not only reshape the physical landscape but also the political and social order. She predicted that nations would struggle to cope with the influx of climate refugees, leading to political instability and conflict over resources. As coastal cities are submerged, populations would be forced to migrate inland, creating competition for land, water, and food. This mass displacement, coupled with the loss of agricultural land due to flooding, would create conditions ripe for conflict. In this sense, her prophecy of the melting ice caps goes beyond environmental disaster—it is a vision of a world on the brink of social and political collapse.

The melting ice caps would also have profound economic consequences. Coastal cities, many of which are major economic hubs, would be particularly vulnerable to rising sea levels. Cities like New York, Tokyo, and London are built along coastlines and rely on their ports and infrastructure to support global trade. In Baba Vanga's prophecy, the submersion of these cities would cripple the global economy, disrupting supply chains and trade networks. The loss of infrastructure and the cost of rebuilding would place an immense financial burden on governments, further exacerbating the crisis.

Despite the catastrophic nature of this prophecy, there is also an implicit warning and a call to action. While Baba Vanga's vision of 2033 paints a bleak picture of the future, it serves as a reminder that humanity still has time to change course. The scientific community has long argued that mitigating the effects of climate change requires immediate action—reducing carbon emissions, transitioning to renewable energy sources, and protecting natural ecosystems. Baba Vanga's prophecy, while dark, offers a glimpse into a future that could still be avoided if decisive steps are taken.

Baba Vanga's prophecy also raises questions about humanity's resilience in the face of environmental collapse. In her vision, while the world would be forever changed by the melting ice caps, humanity would endure. The survivors would be forced to adapt to new realities, finding ways to live in a world reshaped by climate change. This theme of resilience and adaptation is a common thread in many of her prophecies, reflecting her belief that while the future may be challenging, it is not without hope. The melting ice caps, she predicted, would bring about a period of great difficulty, but they would also force humanity to innovate and find new ways to survive.

As the year 2033 approaches, Baba Vanga's climate warning feels more urgent than ever. The threat of melting ice caps and rising sea levels is no longer confined to the realm of prophecy—it is a real and pressing issue that scientists and policymakers are grappling with today. Whether her prediction for that specific year comes true or not, the underlying message is clear: the window for preventing catastrophic climate change is closing, and the choices humanity makes now will determine the future of the planet.

In this chapter, Baba Vanga's warning about the melting ice caps serves as both a prophecy and a cautionary tale. Her vision of a world submerged by rising seas is a stark reminder of the fragility of our planet's ecosystems and the dire consequences of environmental neglect. As we move closer to 2033, her prophecy stands as a call to action, urging us to confront the realities of climate change before it is too late. Whether her vision becomes reality depends, in part, on humanity's willingness to take bold and decisive action to protect the planet and its future.

A Return to Communism: The World in 2076

Among Baba Vanga's most intriguing and controversial predictions is her prophecy of a global return to communism in the year 2076. This prediction, while puzzling to many, reflects her broader visions of political and social upheaval in the coming centuries. According to her, by 2076, communism would once again rise, not only in the countries that had experienced it in the 20th century, but on a global scale. This worldwide shift toward communism would represent a significant realignment of political systems, social structures, and economic models.

To understand the context of Baba Vanga's prediction, it's important to remember that she lived much of her life under communist rule in Bulgaria, which was part of the Eastern Bloc during the Cold War. Her experiences during this time may have influenced her visions of a future in which communism would return. However, the communism she predicted for 2076 was not simply a revival of the past. Instead, she described it as a new, more evolved form of communism—one that would address the inequalities and challenges of the modern world.

The 20th century saw communism rise and fall in various parts of the world, from the Soviet Union and China to Eastern Europe and Cuba. While some saw communism as a path toward equality and justice, others experienced it as a system of repression and economic failure. By the end of the century, many communist regimes had collapsed, with the fall of the Soviet Union in 1991 marking a definitive end to the Cold War. For Baba Vanga to predict the return of communism, and on a global scale no less, seems at odds with the trajectory of history. However, her prophecy suggests that the conditions that led to the rise of communism in the past—inequality, social unrest, and economic disparity—would once again come to the forefront by 2076.

In Baba Vanga's vision, this new wave of communism would emerge as a response to global crises. She predicted that by the middle of the 21st century, the world would face severe challenges, including economic collapse, environmental disasters, and widespread inequality. These conditions would lead to a rejection of capitalist systems and a collective turn toward a more communal, centralized way of organizing society. While capitalism had dominated much of the world throughout the 20th and early 21st centuries, Baba Vanga believed that it would ultimately fail to address the needs of the global population, particularly in the face of growing resource scarcity and climate change.

Baba Vanga's prediction suggests that the new form of communism would not be imposed by a single country or ideology but would emerge organically as nations and societies sought solutions to their problems. In her vision, this shift would be driven by the need for collective action to solve global issues such as climate change, inequality, and the depletion of natural resources. As nations struggled to cope with these challenges, the idea of shared ownership of resources, centralized planning, and collective decision-making would gain popularity.

IN MANY WAYS, BABA Vanga's prophecy of communism in 2076 reflects concerns that are already being debated in the modern world. The growing gap between the rich and the poor, the concentration of wealth in the hands of a few, and the environmental destruction caused by unchecked capitalism have led to increasing calls for systemic change. Movements for social and economic justice, such as the push for universal basic income, environmental sustainability, and wealth redistribution, echo the ideals of equality and shared prosperity that communism espouses. In this sense, Baba Vanga's prophecy may be seen as an extension of these ongoing debates, envisioning a future where these ideas are fully realized on a global scale.

However, Baba Vanga's prediction also raises important questions about the nature of this new form of communism. Would it mirror the authoritarian regimes of the 20th century, or would it represent a more democratic and egalitarian model? In her vision, the new communism was not necessarily tied to the repressive state control seen in past communist governments. Instead, she described it as a system that would evolve to meet the needs of the time, one that prioritized social welfare, environmental protection, and the equitable distribution of resources. This vision aligns with some contemporary discussions around eco-socialism and green communism, ideologies that seek to combine environmental sustainability with social justice.

While Baba Vanga's prophecy of communism in 2076 is intriguing, it is also met with skepticism. Many argue that communism, as an economic and political system, has been discredited by its failures in the 20th century, particularly in places like the Soviet Union, where it led to widespread poverty, repression, and political corruption. The collapse of communism in Eastern Europe and the shift toward market economies in China and Vietnam seem to indicate that the world has moved past the idea of communism as a viable system. Yet, Baba Vanga's vision suggests that history may be cyclical, and that the failures of capitalism in the future could lead to a resurgence of communist ideals.

One possible interpretation of Baba Vanga's prediction is that it reflects a broader trend toward collectivism in response to global challenges. As the world faces unprecedented crises—such as climate change, pandemics, and economic inequality—there is a growing recognition that individual nations cannot solve these problems alone. International cooperation, shared resources, and collective action are becoming increasingly necessary to address global issues. In this context, the rise of a new form of communism could be seen as a metaphor for the shift toward more collective and cooperative solutions to the world's problems.

Baba Vanga's prophecy of a return to communism also invites reflection on the future of global governance. As the world becomes more interconnected, traditional nation-states may struggle to address the complex challenges of the 21st century. In her vision, the rise of communism in 2076 could be linked to a new form of global governance, where nations pool their resources and work together to solve problems. This would represent a significant departure from the competitive, nationalist politics of today and could lead to a more unified, cooperative world.

Despite the utopian aspects of Baba Vanga's prediction, her vision also contains a cautionary element. The rise of communism in 2076, according to her, would not come without struggle. She foresaw a period of conflict and upheaval as old systems of power were dismantled and new ones emerged. The transition to a global communist system, she predicted, would be marked by political unrest, economic challenges, and resistance from those who stood to lose power and wealth. This vision suggests that the path to a new world order, while necessary, would not be an easy one.

As we look toward the future, Baba Vanga's prophecy of a return to communism in 2076 invites us to consider the trajectory of our current political and economic systems. While the idea of global communism may seem unlikely today, the underlying concerns about inequality, environmental degradation, and social justice are very real. Whether or not her prediction comes to pass, it reflects the growing sense that the status quo is unsustainable and that new solutions will be needed to address the challenges of the future. In this way, Baba Vanga's vision of 2076 offers both a warning and a glimpse of what may lie ahead.

Alien Encounters: 2130 and Humanity's Cosmic Connection

One of the more fantastical and captivating predictions made by Baba Vanga is her prophecy regarding the year 2130, when humanity is said to make contact with extraterrestrial life. According to Baba Vanga, this event would be a defining moment in human history—our first encounter with beings from beyond Earth. While many of her prophecies deal with the material struggles of life on our planet, this particular vision points to something much grander: the expansion of human consciousness and understanding of our place in the universe.

Baba Vanga's prophecy of alien contact in 2130 speaks to a deeply ingrained human fascination with the cosmos and the possibility of life beyond Earth. For centuries, the idea that we are not alone in the universe has captured the imagination of scientists, philosophers, and the general public alike. The search for extraterrestrial intelligence (SETI), along with numerous space exploration missions, reflects this enduring curiosity. Yet, despite decades of searching, humanity has not yet discovered definitive proof of alien life. Baba Vanga's vision, however, suggests that by 2130, this will change.

In her prophecy, Baba Vanga predicted that humans would not only make contact with extraterrestrial beings but also collaborate with them, marking the beginning of a new era of cooperation between species. This cosmic connection, as she foresaw it, would revolutionize our understanding of science, technology, and spirituality. The knowledge and wisdom imparted by these advanced beings would help humanity overcome many of the challenges it faces, particularly those related to environmental degradation, energy shortages, and conflict. For Baba Vanga's followers, this prophecy holds out hope for a future where humanity can transcend its limitations and reach new heights of achievement through this cosmic partnership.

While Baba Vanga did not provide specific details about the nature of these extraterrestrial beings, her vision aligns with a broader cultural narrative about intelligent life in the universe. Over the years, scientists have speculated about the existence of alien civilizations, pointing to the sheer size of the cosmos as evidence that it is highly likely life exists elsewhere. The discovery of exoplanets—planets orbiting other stars—has only fueled this speculation, as many of these planets lie within the "habitable zone," where conditions could potentially support life. Baba Vanga's prophecy taps into this scientific curiosity, suggesting that the answer to the age-old question of "Are we alone?" will finally be revealed in the 22nd century.

Baba Vanga's prediction of alien contact is not entirely unique. Throughout history, numerous prophets, mystics, and even modern-day scientists have speculated about the possibility of human encounters with extraterrestrial life. What sets her prophecy apart is the emphasis she placed on the positive nature of this contact. In contrast to many popular depictions of alien invasions or hostile encounters, Baba Vanga's vision suggests that these beings would come not as conquerors, but as collaborators—offering their knowledge and technology to help humanity advance.

In her vision, this encounter with extraterrestrials would not only lead to technological advancements but also spark a profound shift in human consciousness. Baba Vanga predicted that the arrival of these beings would challenge humanity's understanding of its place in the cosmos, prompting philosophical and spiritual awakenings. As humans grapple with the realization that we are not alone, our collective worldview would expand, leading to a deeper sense of connection to the universe and to one another. This cosmic revelation, she believed, would help humanity overcome its divisions, fostering a sense of unity and purpose on a global scale.

The idea that alien contact could serve as a catalyst for human evolution is a theme that resonates with many modern thinkers. In science fiction and speculative philosophy, the concept of humanity "graduating" to a higher level of existence through contact with advanced civilizations is a common trope. Baba Vanga's prophecy seems to align with this idea, suggesting that extraterrestrials would play a pivotal role in guiding humanity toward a more enlightened future. Their knowledge of advanced technologies, such as sustainable energy, space travel, and even possibly interdimensional understanding, would be shared with humanity, allowing us to solve many of the existential problems we face today.

While Baba Vanga's prophecy offers a hopeful vision of humanity's future, it also raises intriguing questions about the nature of these extraterrestrial beings. What would they look like? How would they communicate with us? What motivations would drive them to reach out to humanity? Baba Vanga did not provide specific answers to these questions, leaving much to the imagination. However, her vision suggests that these beings would be vastly more advanced than humans, both technologically and spiritually, and would have an interest in helping humanity evolve rather than dominating or exploiting us.

Interestingly, Baba Vanga's prophecy of alien contact in 2130 coincides with predictions from other sources about humanity's increasing involvement in space exploration. By the 22nd century, it is likely that humans will have established permanent colonies on the Moon, Mars, and possibly other celestial bodies. Our technological capabilities will have expanded, and our ability to explore deeper into the universe will be far greater than it is today. In this context, the idea that we might encounter extraterrestrial life becomes more plausible. As we reach out into the stars, we may find that other civilizations have been waiting for us to develop the means to make contact.

The prophecy also raises questions about how humanity will respond to the discovery of extraterrestrial life. Would this encounter lead to a period of cooperation and enlightenment, as Baba Vanga predicted, or would it spark fear, conflict, and division? The answer likely depends on the state of humanity at the time. If we are able to overcome our internal divisions and approach this cosmic encounter with an open mind, it could lead to an era of unprecedented progress. However, if humanity is still mired in conflict, inequality, and environmental degradation, the arrival of extraterrestrial beings could exacerbate these issues.

In many ways, Baba Vanga's prophecy of alien contact is both a hopeful and cautionary tale. It offers the promise of technological and spiritual advancement, but it also reminds us of the importance of preparing for such an encounter. Humanity must evolve not just technologically, but morally and spiritually, to be ready for the profound changes that alien contact would bring. In her vision, the extraterrestrials come to guide humanity, but it is up to us to determine how we respond to their presence.

As the year 2130 approaches, the idea of alien contact will likely continue to capture the imagination of people around the world. Baba Vanga's prophecy offers a tantalizing glimpse into a future where humanity is no longer confined to Earth, but is part of a larger cosmic community. Whether or not this prophecy comes true, it reflects the deep longing within humanity to connect with something greater than ourselves—whether that be other civilizations, or a deeper understanding of the universe itself.

In this chapter, we explore Baba Vanga's vision of alien encounters in 2130, a prophecy that suggests a future where humanity's horizons expand far beyond our current understanding. As we continue to search the stars and push the boundaries of science, her prophecy reminds us of the potential for discovery and transformation that lies ahead—both in the universe and within ourselves.

Drought and Despair: The Global Crisis of 2170

One of Baba Vanga's most foreboding predictions deals with a worldwide drought in the year 2170, a crisis that would bring humanity to the brink of collapse. According to her prophecy, this devastating drought would sweep across the planet, plunging nations into a state of despair as water sources dried up, crops failed, and entire ecosystems crumbled. This vision of the future aligns with concerns already expressed by modern scientists and environmentalists, who warn of the catastrophic consequences of climate change and its potential to disrupt global water supplies. In this chapter, we will explore Baba Vanga's vision of the global drought of 2170 and its potential implications for the survival of humanity.

Baba Vanga's prediction of a severe drought is not unique to her; many contemporary climate models predict that by the late 21st and early 22nd centuries, water shortages could become one of the most pressing global challenges. Rising temperatures, changing weather patterns, and the overuse of freshwater resources are expected to cause widespread droughts in regions that rely heavily on agriculture and consistent rainfall. According to her prophecy, by 2170, these environmental pressures will have reached a tipping point, with large swaths of the planet becoming inhospitable due to the lack of water.

The consequences of such a global drought would be far-reaching and devastating. Water, after all, is essential not only for human survival but for every ecosystem on the planet. In Baba Vanga's vision, as the drought deepens, rivers dry up, reservoirs are depleted, and the agricultural systems that support billions of people collapse. Crops fail, livestock perish, and food shortages become widespread. In her prophecy, the world plunges into chaos as governments struggle to manage the growing crisis, leading to conflict, social unrest, and mass migration as populations flee drought-stricken regions in search of water and fertile land.

Baba Vanga's prediction of a world gripped by drought reflects a broader theme in her prophecies: the vulnerability of humanity to environmental collapse. Her vision of the future warns not only of the physical devastation caused by drought but also of the social and political consequences. As nations struggle to provide for their citizens, tensions over dwindling resources will likely rise, leading to conflict between countries and even within them. Wars over water rights, territory, and food supplies could become commonplace, further destabilizing regions already weakened by the effects of climate change.

While Baba Vanga's prophecy may seem extreme, the idea of drought leading to global chaos is not far-fetched. Modern scientists have already observed the impact of prolonged droughts in various regions of the world. In places like the Middle East, Africa, and parts of South Asia, water scarcity has been linked to food insecurity, migration, and even conflict. For example, the Syrian civil war, which began in 2011, has been partially attributed to a severe drought that hit the country between 2006 and 2011, leading to crop failures, economic hardship, and mass displacement of rural populations. These types of crises, which are currently limited to specific regions, could become more widespread by 2170 if climate change continues unchecked.

In her prophecy, Baba Vanga also foresaw that the global drought would lead to unprecedented technological and scientific efforts to address the crisis. Humanity, she believed, would be forced to innovate and develop new methods for water conservation, purification, and production. In her vision, the drought serves as a wake-up call, pushing the world's brightest minds to find solutions to the water shortage. These advancements, while initially developed to manage the immediate crisis, would ultimately lead to breakthroughs in water management and agricultural technologies that could reshape the future of human civilization.

Some scientists and engineers are already exploring potential solutions to the global water crisis, and Baba Vanga's prophecy of technological innovation aligns with these efforts. Desalination, the process of removing salt from seawater, has been proposed as a solution for regions facing freshwater shortages. However, the energy-intensive nature of desalination and the environmental impact of disposing of the leftover brine make it an imperfect solution. Similarly, advancements in water recycling, irrigation technology, and drought-resistant crops are being explored as ways to combat water scarcity in the coming decades. Baba Vanga's vision suggests that by 2170, these technologies will be essential for human survival.

However, her prophecy also implies that these technological solutions may come too late to prevent the widespread suffering caused by the drought. In her vision, the crisis of 2170 is a reminder of humanity's failure to heed earlier warnings about environmental degradation and the unsustainable use of natural resources. The drought, in this sense, is both a consequence of human negligence and a catalyst for change. Baba Vanga's followers interpret this prophecy as a call to action—a warning that unless humanity changes its ways and addresses the root causes of climate change, the world will face irreversible damage.

Baba Vanga's prophecy also touches on the political dimensions of the global drought. She predicted that as water becomes scarcer, new systems of governance would emerge to manage the allocation and distribution of resources. In her vision, centralized control over water supplies would become necessary, leading to the rise of powerful institutions or even global authorities tasked with regulating access to water. These entities, she believed, would wield significant influence over the world's population, potentially leading to tensions between those who control the water and those who depend on it.

This vision of centralized control over water resources raises important ethical and political questions. Who will have access to water in a world where it is scarce? Will wealthy nations and individuals hoard resources, leaving poorer populations to suffer? Or will humanity find a way to equitably distribute water and ensure that it remains a public good rather than a commodity? Baba Vanga's prophecy offers no clear answers but suggests that the political dynamics surrounding water will be a critical issue in the 22nd century.

THE DROUGHT OF 2170, as foreseen by Baba Vanga, represents more than just an environmental disaster—it is a symbol of humanity's vulnerability to the forces of nature and the consequences of our actions. Her vision serves as a stark reminder that the choices we make today regarding resource management, environmental protection, and sustainability will have profound effects on future generations. While the drought she predicted may seem distant, the warning it carries is relevant to our present moment. The signs of environmental collapse are already visible, and the need for action has never been more urgent.

In this chapter, Baba Vanga's prophecy of a global drought in 2170 serves as both a prediction and a cautionary tale. It is a vision of a world where the failure to address environmental challenges leads to widespread suffering, conflict, and despair. At the same time, it is also a call to action, urging humanity to take responsibility for the planet and to innovate in ways that ensure a sustainable future. Whether or not her prophecy comes to pass, the message it conveys is clear: the choices we make today will shape the world of tomorrow. If we continue on our current path, the drought and despair of 2170 may be closer than we think.

The Martian War: The Future Battle for Mars in 3005

Baba Vanga's prophecies often delve into the mysterious and the unknown, but few of her predictions are as far-reaching and speculative as the one concerning a future war on Mars. According to her, in the year 3005, humanity will find itself embroiled in a conflict with a civilization on Mars—whether that civilization will be human or extraterrestrial remains unclear. This prophecy, filled with images of cosmic battles and technological warfare, paints a picture of a future where humanity has expanded beyond Earth but faces new, unforeseen dangers in the vastness of space.

The idea of a Martian war in the distant future taps into some of the deepest and most enduring themes in science fiction: space exploration, extraterrestrial life, and the potential for conflict between worlds. While Baba Vanga's prediction may seem far-fetched today, especially in light of our current understanding of Mars as a barren, inhospitable planet, the rapid advancements in space technology and the increasing focus on Mars as a potential target for colonization suggest that this scenario might not be entirely outside the realm of possibility.

In recent years, Mars has become a focal point for space exploration, with NASA, the European Space Agency (ESA), and private companies like SpaceX making significant strides toward the goal of sending humans to the Red Planet. While the initial goal of these missions is exploration and the establishment of human colonies, Baba Vanga's prophecy suggests that Mars will eventually become a battleground—one where humanity's survival and dominance in space may be at stake.

According to Baba Vanga's vision, by the year 3005, humanity will have established a significant presence on Mars, either through colonization or as part of a broader cosmic expansion. This presence, however, will not go unchallenged. Her prophecy hints at the existence of a civilization on Mars—whether it is native to the planet or an extraterrestrial force that has taken up residence there remains ambiguous. What is clear from her vision is that this civilization will come into conflict with humanity, leading to a war that spans across the solar system.

The nature of this war, as described by Baba Vanga, suggests that it will be unlike any conflict humanity has experienced on Earth. The technologies involved will be highly advanced, incorporating innovations in space travel, energy weapons, and possibly artificial intelligence. Battles will take place not only on the surface of Mars but also in orbit and across interplanetary distances. This futuristic warfare will challenge humanity's understanding of combat, strategy, and survival, as the stakes will be nothing less than control over the future of the planet—and perhaps the solar system itself.

One of the most intriguing aspects of Baba Vanga's prophecy is the question of who, or what, this Martian civilization might be. Mars, as we understand it today, is a cold, desolate world with no evidence of intelligent life. However, in Baba Vanga's vision, Mars in the year 3005 is inhabited by a formidable force capable of waging war against humanity. This raises several possibilities. Could this Martian civilization be an ancient, hidden race that has existed on the planet for millennia, waiting for the right moment to reveal itself? Or could it be an extraterrestrial species that has colonized Mars after migrating from another star system?

Alternatively, Baba Vanga's prophecy may not refer to an alien species at all, but rather to a conflict between human factions. By 3005, humanity may have spread across multiple planets and moons, developing distinct cultures, political systems, and ideologies. The war on Mars could represent a civil war between different human colonies, each vying for control over the planet's resources or strategic location in the solar system. In this scenario, the Martian war would be an extension of humanity's long history of territorial conflict, only this time, the stakes would be interplanetary.

Regardless of who the opposing force is, Baba Vanga's prophecy suggests that the Martian war will have far-reaching consequences for both Earth and Mars. The conflict may start as a localized struggle for control over Martian resources—such as water, minerals, or even advanced technology—but it will quickly escalate into a larger battle that threatens the stability of the entire solar system. In her vision, this war will be a turning point in human history, forcing humanity to confront the reality of life beyond Earth and the challenges that come with cosmic expansion.

The idea of a Martian war also raises questions about humanity's future role in space. As we continue to explore and colonize other planets, will we bring our conflicts and divisions with us? Will the same political, economic, and social struggles that have shaped human history on Earth carry over to our interactions with other worlds? Baba Vanga's prophecy seems to suggest that even in the distant future, humanity's propensity for conflict will persist, threatening to disrupt our progress and achievements in space.

At the same time, the prophecy offers a glimpse into the potential for growth and evolution. While the war on Mars may be a period of great destruction, it could also serve as a catalyst for technological and social advancements. Just as wars on Earth have often led to periods of innovation—spurring the development of new technologies, medical breakthroughs, and shifts in political power—the Martian war could drive humanity to new heights of achievement. The need to survive and prevail in this interplanetary conflict might push humanity to develop new forms of energy, space travel, and communication that could reshape the future of life in the solar system.

In Baba Vanga's vision, the war on Mars is not just a conflict between two civilizations or factions—it is a test of humanity's ability to adapt, innovate, and survive in the cosmos. The war will challenge humanity's understanding of its place in the universe, forcing us to confront questions about the ethics of space colonization, the potential for peaceful coexistence with other civilizations, and the limits of human ambition.

While Baba Vanga's prophecy may seem distant and speculative, it reflects real-world concerns about the future of space exploration and the possibility of conflict beyond Earth. As humanity takes its first steps toward becoming a multi-planetary species, the potential for competition, resource scarcity, and territorial disputes looms large. The dream of colonizing other planets is often framed in utopian terms, with visions of a united humanity working together to explore the stars. However, Baba Vanga's prophecy reminds us that the realities of space colonization may be far more complex and fraught with danger.

As we look toward the distant future, the possibility of a Martian war in 3005 invites us to consider the ethical, political, and technological challenges of expanding beyond Earth. Will humanity learn from its past mistakes and find a way to peacefully coexist with other civilizations, both human and extraterrestrial? Or will the same forces that have driven conflict on Earth follow us into the stars? Baba Vanga's prophecy offers no clear answers, but it serves as a cautionary tale, reminding us that the future of space exploration will be shaped not only by our technological capabilities but also by our capacity for cooperation, understanding, and conflict resolution.

In this chapter, Baba Vanga's prediction of the Martian war in 3005 serves as a stark reminder of the potential challenges that lie ahead as humanity ventures into the cosmos. Whether the conflict is with extraterrestrial beings or fellow humans, the war on Mars will test humanity's ability to adapt to a new frontier. As we continue to push the boundaries of space exploration, her prophecy invites us to reflect on the possibilities and perils of expanding beyond our home planet—and the lessons we must carry with us as we explore the final frontier.

Human Exodus: Evacuating Earth in 3797

One of Baba Vanga's most dramatic and far-reaching prophecies involves the complete evacuation of Earth in the year 3797. According to her vision, by this time, Earth will no longer be able to support human life, forcing the remaining population to leave the planet in search of a new home. This massive exodus, driven by environmental collapse and the depletion of resources, represents one of the most significant moments in human history—an event that will mark the end of humanity's long-standing connection to its home planet and the beginning of a new chapter in the cosmos.

The idea of humans leaving Earth, whether by necessity or choice, has long been a theme in both science fiction and futurist thought. While space exploration today is focused on expanding humanity's presence beyond Earth through colonization of nearby planets like Mars or the Moon, Baba Vanga's prophecy suggests a much more dire scenario—one where humanity has no choice but to abandon Earth entirely. The notion of evacuating the planet is not only a commentary on environmental degradation but also an exploration of the resilience and adaptability of the human species in the face of existential threats.

Baba Vanga's prophecy of the human exodus in 3797 paints a bleak picture of Earth's future. By this time, the planet will have become uninhabitable, its resources depleted and its ecosystems destroyed. Whether due to climate change, nuclear disaster, asteroid impact, or other catastrophic events, Earth will no longer be able to sustain human life. The remaining population, unable to reverse the damage, will be forced to seek refuge in the stars, using advanced spacefaring technology to find new worlds that can support them.

This prediction reflects a growing awareness in today's world about the limits of Earth's resources and the environmental consequences of unchecked human activity. Scientists and environmentalists have long warned that the planet's ecosystems are fragile, and that continued exploitation of natural resources, coupled with the effects of climate change, could lead to a point of no return. While efforts are being made to combat climate change and develop sustainable technologies, Baba Vanga's prophecy suggests that these efforts may ultimately fall short, leading to the collapse of Earth's ability to sustain life by the 38th century.

The exodus from Earth, as foreseen by Baba Vanga, would not be a spontaneous event but the result of centuries of preparation. Humanity would have developed the technology to travel to distant star systems, with the knowledge that Earth's decline was inevitable. This suggests a future where space exploration and colonization are no longer dreams of the distant future but a reality that has been in place for centuries by the time of the exodus. By 3797, space travel would be sophisticated enough to transport large numbers of people across interstellar distances, and the search for habitable planets would have already been underway for generations.

IN HER VISION, THE human exodus is not just a matter of survival but also a test of humanity's ingenuity and perseverance. Baba Vanga foresaw that while Earth would be lost, humanity would endure. The people who leave Earth behind would carry with them the knowledge, culture, and history of their ancestors, preserving the legacy of human civilization as they search for a new home. This theme of survival and continuity runs through many of Baba Vanga's prophecies, emphasizing the resilience of the human spirit even in the face of overwhelming challenges.

The logistics of such a mass evacuation would be staggering. By 3797, Earth's population may have reached trillions, depending on advancements in technology, medicine, and space colonization. While Baba Vanga's prophecy does not specify the exact details of how the exodus would take place, it is clear that humanity would rely on vast fleets of spacecraft capable of supporting life for long journeys through space. These ships, likely equipped with artificial ecosystems, advanced propulsion systems, and life-sustaining technologies, would serve as temporary homes for the evacuees as they search for habitable planets.

Baba Vanga's vision of a human exodus also raises important questions about the ethical and social implications of abandoning Earth. Who will be chosen to leave? Will the evacuation be a democratic process, or will it be controlled by a select few with the resources and power to secure their passage off the planet? The evacuation of Earth could exacerbate existing inequalities, with the wealthy and powerful gaining access to space travel while the poor and marginalized are left behind. Alternatively, it could be a moment of unity, where humanity comes together to ensure the survival of the species as a whole.

In Baba Vanga's vision, the human exodus is not the end of the story. After leaving Earth, humanity will embark on a journey through the stars, seeking a new planet to call home. The search for a habitable world will likely take generations, and the challenges of surviving in space will test the limits of human endurance and innovation. As humans travel through the cosmos, they will encounter new environments, possibly even new forms of life. This cosmic journey represents a new phase in human evolution, where the species is no longer bound to its home planet but becomes a spacefaring civilization.

The idea of humanity leaving Earth and becoming an interstellar species has fascinated futurists for decades. Visionaries like Elon Musk have proposed colonizing Mars as a backup plan in case Earth becomes uninhabitable. Others have suggested that humanity's long-term survival may depend on our ability to find and colonize planets outside our solar system. Baba Vanga's prophecy takes this concept to its logical extreme, suggesting that the day will come when Earth is no longer viable, and humanity must move on.

WHILE THE NOTION OF a human exodus from Earth may seem distant and speculative, it is rooted in real-world concerns about the future of our planet. Climate change, overpopulation, and the depletion of natural resources are already placing immense pressure on Earth's ecosystems. If these trends continue, humanity may face difficult choices about how to ensure its survival. Baba Vanga's prophecy of the exodus in 3797 serves as both a warning and a glimpse into a potential future where the limits of Earth's capacity to support life are reached, and humanity is forced to seek new horizons.

Interestingly, Baba Vanga's vision of a human exodus is not one of despair but of hope. While the loss of Earth is tragic, her prophecy emphasizes humanity's resilience and ability to adapt to new challenges. The people who leave Earth will carry with them the knowledge and culture of the planet, ensuring that human civilization continues to thrive even in the face of cosmic adversity. In this sense, the exodus is not an ending but a new beginning—a chance for humanity to explore the stars and create new worlds.

As we look toward the distant future, Baba Vanga's prophecy of the human exodus in 3797 invites us to reflect on the current state of our planet and the choices we make today. While the idea of evacuating Earth may seem far off, the underlying message of her prophecy is clear: humanity's survival depends on our ability to recognize and address the environmental and social challenges we face. If we fail to protect our planet, the day may come when we have no choice but to leave it behind.

In this chapter, Baba Vanga's vision of the human exodus serves as a powerful reminder of both the fragility of our planet and the resilience of the human spirit. The evacuation of Earth in 3797 represents a turning point in human history, one that challenges us to think about the future of our species and our place in the universe. As we continue to explore space and push the boundaries of science and technology, her prophecy encourages us to consider what it means to be human—and what it will take to survive in a changing world.

Chapter 15: The Final Year: The End of the World in 5079

Among Baba Vanga's vast array of prophecies, her prediction for the year 5079 stands as the most final and ominous: the end of the world. According to her, this is the year in which humanity will face its ultimate conclusion, marking the end of Earth, life as we know it, and possibly the universe itself. While her earlier prophecies predict wars, natural disasters, and human resilience, this particular vision offers no such hope. In Baba Vanga's vision, 5079 is the last chapter in the story of humanity—a year when everything ceases to exist.

The prophecy of the world's end in 5079 is both mysterious and chilling. Baba Vanga, who often spoke in terms of human survival and adaptation, saw this date as an inevitable conclusion to the long arc of human history. In her vision, there was no escaping the end, no exodus to distant planets, no new civilizations rising from the ashes—just a final, irreversible end. What exactly causes this end is not entirely clear in her prophecies, but the mere existence of such a specific year invites contemplation about what could lead to the annihilation of everything.

One of the most intriguing aspects of this prophecy is its focus on a date so far in the future that it stretches beyond our current understanding of science, technology, and human potential. The year 5079 is far removed from the crises and challenges we face today, offering a glimpse into a time when humanity may have evolved far beyond our present state. By then, if Baba Vanga's other predictions are to be believed, humans will have mastered space travel, created advanced technologies, and may even have established civilizations on other planets or beyond the solar system. And yet, despite all of these advancements, her prophecy suggests that there is an endpoint—a final moment when all of this progress will be undone.

While Baba Vanga did not provide a detailed explanation for how the world will end in 5079, her vision leaves room for speculation. The end could come from a variety of sources, including natural cosmic events, human-caused disasters, or even forces beyond our current comprehension. One possibility is that the end could be triggered by a cosmic event, such as the collision of galaxies, a supernova, or the death of the Sun. Astrophysicists have long predicted that in several billion years, the Sun will exhaust its nuclear fuel, expanding into a red giant and potentially engulfing the Earth. By 5079, such cosmic forces could be in play, leading to the destruction of our planet and possibly even the solar system.

Alternatively, the end of the world could come from humanity itself. Throughout history, humans have demonstrated a capacity for both great creation and great destruction. As we continue to develop increasingly powerful technologies—such as artificial intelligence, nuclear energy, and genetic engineering—the potential for catastrophic mistakes grows. A technological disaster, whether intentional or accidental, could bring about the end of civilization or even life on Earth. The distant year of 5079 might see the culmination of these destructive tendencies, resulting in an apocalypse brought on by human innovation gone awry.

Another possibility is that Baba Vanga's prophecy refers not just to the end of Earth or humanity, but to the end of the universe itself. Modern physics presents us with several theories about the ultimate fate of the universe, including the possibility of heat death, where the universe reaches a state of maximum entropy and all energy becomes evenly distributed, making life and movement impossible. There are also theories about the Big Rip, in which the universe's expansion accelerates to the point where all matter is torn apart, or the Big Crunch, where the universe collapses in on itself. If Baba Vanga's prophecy aligns with any of these scientific theories, the year 5079 could mark the moment when the universe itself ceases to exist.

Despite the grim nature of this prophecy, it is also a moment for reflection on the nature of time, existence, and the meaning of life. If the world is indeed destined to end in 5079, what does that mean for humanity today? Baba Vanga's prediction invites us to think about the legacy we leave behind, the progress we make, and the purpose of our lives in the face of such an eventual endpoint. While the idea of an absolute end may seem frightening, it also offers a certain clarity—an understanding that everything, even the universe itself, is finite.

The prophecy also raises existential questions about the role of humanity in the cosmos. If the end is inevitable, how do we define our significance in the grand scheme of things? Does the knowledge that the world will eventually end diminish the importance of our actions, or does it make our time on Earth even more meaningful? Baba Vanga's vision of the final year challenges us to consider the nature of existence itself and our place within it. Are we simply a fleeting moment in an infinite cosmos, or do our lives and contributions have a lasting impact, even in the face of oblivion?

In many ways, the prophecy of the end of the world in 5079 serves as a reminder of the fragility of life and the impermanence of all things. Just as individual lives come to an end, so too does the planet, and perhaps the universe. This recognition of impermanence can inspire us to live with greater awareness, compassion, and purpose. If the end is inevitable, then the time we have now becomes even more precious. Baba Vanga's prophecy urges us to think about how we use that time—whether we spend it in conflict and destruction or in creation and growth.

The prophecy of 5079 also prompts us to consider the future of human civilization. Even if the end is inevitable, what will the world look like in the centuries leading up to that moment? Baba Vanga's other predictions suggest that humanity will achieve incredible technological and scientific advancements, from colonizing other planets to making contact with extraterrestrial beings. By the time 5079 arrives, humans may be living in ways we cannot even imagine today, with technologies that extend life, enhance intelligence, and explore the deepest mysteries of the universe.

However, this progress may ultimately be meaningless in the face of the end. Baba Vanga's prophecy reminds us that no matter how advanced we become, no matter how far we travel or how much we discover, there will always be forces beyond our control—forces that can bring everything to an end. This humbling realization invites us to approach the future with both optimism and humility, recognizing the limits of human power and the inevitability of change.

In this final chapter, Baba Vanga's vision of the end of the world in 5079 serves as both a conclusion to her prophecies and a profound meditation on the nature of existence. While her earlier predictions focus on survival, adaptation, and resilience, this prophecy acknowledges the ultimate reality that all things must come to an end. Whether this end comes from cosmic forces, human actions, or the natural evolution of the universe, Baba Vanga's prophecy challenges us to confront the unknown with both curiosity and acceptance.

As we look toward the distant future, the prophecy of 5079 encourages us to reflect on the meaning of our lives, our civilizations, and our contributions to the universe. While the end may be inevitable, the journey toward that moment is filled with opportunities for growth, discovery, and connection. In this way, Baba Vanga's vision of the final year becomes not just a prediction of doom, but a reminder to live fully, knowing that even in the face of the ultimate end, the choices we make today shape the legacy we leave behind.

Baba Vanga's Prophecies of the 21st Century

Baba Vanga's prophecies for the 21st century are some of the most intriguing and closely scrutinized, given that they relate to events within a timeframe familiar to us. Her predictions for this century cover a wide range of topics, from political upheavals and environmental disasters to scientific breakthroughs and societal shifts. These prophecies have sparked both fascination and debate, with some believers pointing to events that appear to align with her predictions, while sceptics question the accuracy and interpretations of her visions. In this chapter, we explore Baba Vanga's most notable prophecies for the 21st century and examine how they reflect the challenges, crises, and advancements humanity faces today.

The 9/11 Terrorist Attacks

One of Baba Vanga's most famous prophecies is said to be her foretelling of the September 11, 2001, attacks in the United States. According to reports, she predicted that "two steel birds" would strike America, leading to massive destruction. Many interpret this as a reference to the two hijacked planes that crashed into the Twin Towers of the World Trade Center in New York. For her followers, this event is a clear example of her prophetic abilities, given the specificity of her description and the global significance of the attack. However, sceptics argue that this interpretation is based on loose symbolism and was only associated with 9/11 after the fact.

The 2004 Indian Ocean Tsunami

Another of Baba Vanga's widely discussed prophecies is her prediction of the 2004 Indian Ocean tsunami, which claimed over 230,000 lives across multiple countries. She is said to have foreseen a "great wave" that would sweep across the shores and bring death and destruction. This vision, according to her followers, aligns closely with the devastating tsunami that occurred after a massive undersea earthquake. While her prediction does seem to correlate with the event, as with many of her prophecies, the lack of specific details and the broad nature of the warning make it difficult to definitively link her vision to this tragedy.

The Rise of ISIS and Global Terrorism

Baba Vanga reportedly predicted the rise of a powerful "caliphate" in the early 21st century, with a reign of terror that would spread across the globe. Many of her followers believe this prophecy refers to the rise of ISIS (the Islamic State of Iraq and Syria) and the wave of terrorist attacks and violent extremism that have taken place across the Middle East, Europe, and other parts of the world. The brutal actions of ISIS, its declaration of a caliphate, and its influence over global terrorism seem to reflect the essence of Baba Vanga's prediction, though again, the details remain open to interpretation.

THE ECONOMIC COLLAPSE of Europe

Baba Vanga predicted significant economic turmoil in Europe during the 21st century, describing a period when the continent would experience severe financial crises and instability. This prophecy gained attention during the 2008 global financial crisis and the subsequent Eurozone debt crisis, which saw several European countries, including Greece, Spain, and Italy, teeter on the brink of economic collapse. The aftershocks of these crises continue to affect European economies today, with rising debt levels, political fragmentation, and social unrest. While her prediction does not pinpoint specific events, the broader themes of economic instability and disunity in Europe seem to resonate with current events.

The 2022 UK Floods

Baba Vanga is also credited with predicting the devastating floods that hit the United Kingdom in 2022, an event that brought severe flooding and damage to multiple regions. The prophecy of "a great deluge in Britain" seemed to align with the heavy rains, rising river levels, and widespread destruction caused by flooding across the UK. Climate scientists have pointed to extreme weather events like these as increasingly common occurrences due to global warming, which ties into Baba Vanga's broader predictions about environmental degradation and climate change throughout the 21st century.

The Assassination of a Prominent Figure

In her prophecies for the 21st century, Baba Vanga reportedly foresaw the assassination of a prominent political figure, which would send shockwaves around the world. While no such event has yet occurred that fully matches this description, her followers remain vigilant, believing that the prophecy may still unfold. Given the volatility of global politics and the ongoing threats to world leaders, this prediction is one that continues to cause speculation and concern.

A Great Economic Crisis

Baba Vanga predicted a "great economic collapse" that would shake the foundations of the global economy in the early 21st century. Some interpret this as a reference to the 2008 financial crisis and the subsequent recession, which caused widespread unemployment, bank failures, and a prolonged period of economic stagnation. Others argue that the prophecy could refer to an even greater financial disaster yet to come, one that could potentially disrupt global markets on a more catastrophic scale. The uncertainty surrounding the global economy, coupled with rising inequality and political instability, has led many to view Baba Vanga's warning as a potential harbinger of future economic challenges.

Climate Change and Environmental Disasters

Baba Vanga's visions for the 21st century included a series of environmental disasters, many of which are attributed to the effects of climate change. She predicted that rising global temperatures would lead to melting polar ice caps, severe flooding, droughts, and famine. These predictions mirror the concerns of modern scientists, who have warned of the devastating consequences of unchecked global warming.

Extreme weather events, such as hurricanes, wildfires, and heatwaves, have become more frequent and intense in recent years, lending credence to her prophecy of environmental catastrophe. Her prediction that the polar ice caps would melt, leading to rising sea levels and coastal destruction, resonates strongly with the current scientific consensus on climate change.

The Emergence of New Diseases

Baba Vanga also predicted the emergence of new diseases and pandemics that would sweep across the world in the 21st century. This prophecy gained renewed attention during the COVID-19 pandemic, which brought global health systems to their knees and caused millions of deaths. While Baba Vanga did not specify the exact nature of the diseases she foresaw, the rapid spread of COVID-19 and the ongoing threat of other emerging infectious diseases align with her broader warning about global health crises. Her prophecy serves as a reminder that humanity's vulnerability to new diseases is a challenge that must be continuously addressed.

Scientific Breakthroughs

Not all of Baba Vanga's prophecies for the 21st century are bleak. She also predicted significant scientific advancements, particularly in medicine and technology. One of her most hopeful predictions is the development of new treatments that will extend human life and potentially cure diseases like cancer. Medical research and advancements in biotechnology, gene editing, and personalized medicine are already making strides in these areas, and Baba Vanga's vision of a future where humans live longer, healthier lives may not be as far-fetched as it once seemed.

Her followers also believe that she predicted the rise of artificial intelligence and its growing role in society. As AI continues to evolve, with advancements in machine learning, automation, and robotics, Baba Vanga's vision of a world transformed by technology appears increasingly prescient. While these technologies hold the potential for great benefit, they also raise ethical questions and concerns about their impact on jobs, privacy, and human autonomy—issues that may have been embedded in Baba Vanga's more cryptic warnings about the future.

Conclusion

Baba Vanga's prophecies for the 21st century touch on some of the most pressing issues of our time, from global terrorism and economic instability to climate change and technological advancement. While some of her predictions have been linked to real-world events, others remain open to interpretation, with their outcomes still unfolding. What remains clear is that Baba Vanga's vision for the 21st century reflects both the hopes and fears of a world in transition—one that is grappling with unprecedented challenges but also striving for progress and survival. As we navigate this century, her prophecies serve as both warnings and inspirations, urging us to confront the crises ahead while also embracing the possibilities that come with scientific and technological innovation. Whether one views her prophecies as divine insights or as interpretations of universal human concerns, they continue to captivate the public imagination and offer a lens through which to reflect on the future we are building today.

Prophetic Accuracy: Truth or Myth?

Baba Vanga's reputation as a mystic and prophet has captivated millions around the world, particularly because of the bold and often unsettling nature of her predictions. While many of her followers swear by her foresight and point to several events that seemingly align with her prophecies, sceptics question the accuracy, validity, and reliability of these predictions. In this chapter, we explore the debate surrounding Baba Vanga's prophetic accuracy, delving into examples of fulfilled prophecies, claims of misinterpretation, and the broader discussion of whether her predictions are rooted in truth or are a product of myth and cultural storytelling.

The Case for Prophetic Accuracy: Fulfilled Predictions

Baba Vanga's supporters argue that her success rate as a prophet is remarkably high, with some estimates suggesting that as many as 85% of her predictions have come true. They often point to specific, high-profile events that seem to directly correspond to her visions:

The 9/11 Attacks: One of the most widely cited examples of Baba Vanga's prophetic accuracy is her alleged prediction of the 9/11 terrorist attacks. Her vision of "two steel birds" crashing into buildings in America is often interpreted as a description of the twin towers being struck by hijacked planes. While sceptics argue that the language is vague and symbolic, believers point to the specific imagery of destruction and the global impact of the event as clear evidence of her foresight.

The 2004 Indian Ocean Tsunami: Another frequently cited prophecy is her prediction of a "great wave" that would cause massive destruction, which many believe refers to the devastating 2004 tsunami. This disaster, caused by a powerful undersea earthquake, resulted in over 230,000 deaths across multiple countries. Baba Vanga's followers interpret her prophecy as being remarkably accurate in describing the nature and scale of the tragedy.

The Rise of ISIS: Baba Vanga reportedly predicted the rise of a "caliphate" that would spread terror and destruction. Her followers claim that this vision aligns with the rise of ISIS in the Middle East and the group's brutal reign of terror. The establishment of ISIS's caliphate and its global impact through terrorism lends weight, in the eyes of believers, to her prophetic abilities.

The Brexit Vote: Another example often highlighted is Baba Vanga's prediction that Europe would face significant upheaval and economic instability in the 21st century. Some interpret this as foreseeing the Brexit vote in 2016, which has caused deep political and economic uncertainty across the continent. Although her prophecies are often more symbolic than precise, supporters argue that the broader themes of division and instability are uncannily accurate.

THE CASE AGAINST PROPHETIC Accuracy: Misinterpretations and Vagueness

While Baba Vanga's prophecies are fascinating, critics argue that many of her predictions are either vague, retroactively applied to events, or simply coincidental. The main points raised by sceptics include:

Vagueness and Symbolism: Many of Baba Vanga's predictions are couched in vague or symbolic language, which allows for multiple interpretations. For example, her description of the "two steel birds" could apply to many different scenarios beyond the 9/11 attacks. Critics argue that prophecies framed in such ambiguous terms can be easily manipulated to fit various events after they occur, a phenomenon known as "retrofitting."

Lack of Verifiable Records: One of the challenges in assessing Baba Vanga's accuracy is the lack of detailed, verifiable records of her predictions. Much of her work was transmitted orally or through second-hand accounts, making it difficult to determine what she truly said. Some of her most famous prophecies, like the prediction of 9/11, were only attributed to her after the event, leading sceptics to question whether these prophecies were altered or exaggerated in hindsight.

Missed Predictions: In addition to the prophecies that allegedly came true, there are several high-profile predictions attributed to Baba Vanga that have not materialized. For example, she predicted that Europe would cease to exist by 2016, which did not happen. Similarly, she foresaw that World War III would break out between 2010 and 2014, which also did not occur. These inaccuracies, according to sceptics, call into question the overall reliability of her predictions.

The Power of Suggestion and Confirmation Bias: Another argument against the belief in Baba Vanga's prophetic abilities is the psychological phenomenon known as confirmation bias. This occurs when people selectively interpret information to confirm their existing beliefs. For example, a person who already believes in Baba Vanga's prophecies may interpret an event like the 2004 tsunami or the rise of ISIS in a way that confirms her predictions, even if the prophecy was initially vague or unrelated. The power of suggestion, especially when combined with cultural narratives of prophecy, can lead people to see patterns and accuracy where there may be none.

Cultural Significance of Prophets

Whether or not one believes in Baba Vanga's prophetic abilities, her impact on culture and collective consciousness is undeniable. Prophets and seers have played a significant role throughout human history, offering guidance, warnings, and hope to societies in times of uncertainty. Baba Vanga, like Nostradamus and Edgar Cayce before her, taps into a deeply ingrained human desire to understand the future and make sense of the world's chaotic events.

For those who believe in her visions, Baba Vanga serves as a bridge between the material world and the spiritual or mystical realm. Her blindness, often seen as a metaphor for her "inner sight," adds to her mystique and enhances her image as a visionary. In cultures where mysticism and prophecy hold spiritual significance, Baba Vanga represents the possibility that there are forces and knowledge beyond human comprehension.

Even for sceptics, Baba Vanga's legacy is a fascinating example of how myths and legends grow around figures who seem to possess extraordinary insight. Her prophecies, whether real or imagined, offer a framework through which people can interpret world events, providing a sense of order and understanding in the face of uncertainty.

Prophecy in a Modern Context

Baba Vanga's prophecies take on new significance in today's rapidly changing world. As technology, climate change, and geopolitical tensions shape the future in unpredictable ways, her visions offer both warnings and reassurance. Whether people interpret her predictions as accurate or symbolic, her prophecies highlight the broader themes that continue to challenge humanity: environmental collapse, global conflict, economic instability, and the search for meaning.

One might argue that the relevance of Baba Vanga's prophecies lies not in their literal accuracy but in their ability to capture the anxieties of the time. In the 21st century, with the pace of change accelerating and the future becoming more uncertain, her predictions—vague and symbolic as they may be—speak to the universal human experience of seeking answers in a complex and often chaotic world.

Truth or Myth? The Legacy of Baba Vanga

Ultimately, the question of whether Baba Vanga's prophecies are truth or myth remains open to interpretation. For believers, her visions are a source of wonder and awe, a testament to the existence of powers beyond the physical world. For sceptics, her prophecies are a fascinating but ultimately flawed reflection of the human tendency to find meaning in ambiguity.

What cannot be denied is Baba Vanga's enduring legacy as one of the most renowned mystics of modern times. Whether her predictions are seen as truth or myth, they continue to captivate and inspire, offering both warnings about the dangers ahead and hope for humanity's resilience. As with all prophetic figures, Baba Vanga's legacy will be shaped by the interpretations and beliefs of those who seek answers in her words, and her place in history as a prophet will likely endure, regardless of the debates about her accuracy.

In this chapter, the exploration of Baba Vanga's prophetic accuracy reveals the complexity of belief, myth, and interpretation. Whether she was a true seer or a symbol of human hope and anxiety, Baba Vanga's visions continue to resonate, inviting us to question what we know, what we believe, and what the future may hold.

Baba Vanga and 9/11: The Prediction that Shocked the World

———

Of all the prophecies attributed to Baba Vanga, none has garnered more attention or controversy than her alleged prediction of the September 11, 2001, terrorist attacks in the United States. Known simply as 9/11, the attack on the World Trade Center in New York City and the Pentagon in Washington, D.C., shocked the world and left a lasting impact on global politics, security, and international relations. For Baba Vanga's followers, her supposed foresight of this tragic event cemented her reputation as a prophet of remarkable accuracy, while sceptics remain unconvinced, attributing the prediction to vague symbolism and retroactive interpretation. In this chapter, we explore the details of Baba Vanga's alleged 9/11 prophecy, its significance, and the ongoing debate surrounding her ability to foresee one of the most devastating events of the 21st century.

The Alleged Prophecy: "Steel Birds" and the Fall of America

Baba Vanga's prediction of 9/11 is often summarized in a single chilling vision: she reportedly foresaw "two steel birds" crashing into the "twin brothers," leading to massive destruction in America. According to her followers, this prophecy is a direct reference to the two planes that crashed into the Twin Towers of the World Trade Center, an interpretation that seems to eerily match the events of that fateful day.

The image of "steel birds" is often seen as a metaphor for airplanes, while the "twin brothers" are interpreted as the Twin Towers. In the aftermath of the attacks, this prophecy gained widespread attention, with many believing that Baba Vanga had foreseen the unprecedented terrorist act years before it occurred. Some accounts suggest she made this prediction as early as the 1980s, adding to the mystique surrounding her abilities.

The visual power of this prophecy—its focus on flight, destruction, and a major symbolic event in American history—has made it one of the most famous predictions attributed to her. For her believers, this prophecy is a clear example of Baba Vanga's ability to see into the future and provide warnings about world-altering events.

A Global Turning Point: The Impact of 9/11

The September 11 attacks marked a pivotal moment in world history. Nearly 3,000 people lost their lives in the coordinated strikes carried out by the terrorist group al-Qaeda. The world watched in shock as the Twin Towers collapsed, and the attacks sparked widespread fear, grief, and confusion. In the years that followed, the event reshaped global politics and security, leading to the War on Terror, military invasions of Afghanistan and Iraq, and significant changes in airport security, intelligence gathering, and counterterrorism efforts.

Given the magnitude of 9/11's impact, it is not surprising that people searched for meaning in the aftermath of such a catastrophe. For Baba Vanga's followers, her prediction of the "steel birds" seemed to offer a profound—if tragic—validation of her prophetic abilities. The event's scale and horror fit with the dramatic nature of her vision, cementing her reputation as a seer capable of foretelling world-changing events.

Critics' Perspective: Coincidence, Symbolism, and Retrofitting

While Baba Vanga's followers view her 9/11 prophecy as one of her most convincing predictions, sceptics offer a different interpretation. Many argue that the language of the prophecy—"steel birds" and "twin brothers"—is too vague to be considered a clear prediction of the attacks. Instead, they suggest that this prophecy is an example of *retrofitting*, a process where ambiguous predictions are interpreted to match specific events after they have occurred.

The image of "steel birds" crashing into "twin brothers" could be applied to a variety of scenarios, not just the 9/11 attacks. Critics point out that, while the interpretation may seem clear in hindsight, there is little evidence that anyone linked Baba Vanga's prophecy to a potential terrorist attack on the Twin Towers before 2001. The fact that the connection was made only after the event occurred weakens the claim that she accurately predicted it in advance.

Additionally, critics argue that the use of metaphor and symbolic language is common in many prophecies, allowing them to be interpreted in multiple ways. Baba Vanga's use of imagery like "birds" and "towers" could have many different meanings, making it difficult to assess the true intent or accuracy of the prediction.

The Role of Symbolism in Prophecy

One of the most significant challenges in evaluating Baba Vanga's 9/11 prophecy is the inherent ambiguity of symbolic language in mystical predictions. Throughout history, prophets and seers have often used metaphors, allegories, and symbols to convey their visions, whether for practical reasons or to obscure their meaning until the right moment. In this context, Baba Vanga's prophecy may be seen as part of a long tradition of mystical foresight expressed through abstract language.

For her followers, the power of symbolism in Baba Vanga's prophecies is not a flaw but a testament to her ability to perceive complex events in ways that transcend literal interpretation. In their view, the metaphor of "steel birds" reflects her deep, intuitive understanding of the future, allowing her to communicate a vision of something as unprecedented as the 9/11 attacks using the language of her time.

However, sceptics argue that the very flexibility of symbolic language makes it easier to link prophecies to events after they occur. Because symbols are open to interpretation, any significant event can be connected to a vague prediction, even if the original intent of the prophecy was unrelated. This flexibility is part of what makes prophetic accuracy so difficult to assess—it is often more about interpretation than concrete foresight.

THE MYSTIQUE OF PROPHECY and Global Events

The 9/11 attacks remain one of the most significant and widely discussed events in modern history. In the wake of such profound tragedy, it is natural for people to seek explanations, whether through political analysis, spiritual reflection, or prophecy. Baba Vanga's vision, with its striking imagery and apparent connection to the attacks, has become part of the cultural narrative surrounding 9/11, adding a layer of mysticism to an event already steeped in historical significance.

For many people, prophecy offers a way to make sense of the chaos and unpredictability of the world. The belief that certain individuals, like Baba Vanga, possess the ability to foresee major events provides comfort and a sense of order in an otherwise uncertain world. Her followers believe that, through her visions, Baba Vanga was able to provide warnings about disasters like 9/11, even if humanity did not act on them in time.

The Enduring Legacy of the 9/11 Prophecy

Whether one believes in Baba Vanga's prophetic abilities or not, her 9/11 prediction has cemented her place in the public consciousness. The striking nature of the imagery and the global impact of the event it is believed to predict have made this vision one of the most enduring examples of her foresight. As with many prophecies, the debate over its accuracy continues, with believers and sceptics offering competing interpretations.

For her followers, Baba Vanga's 9/11 prophecy is a powerful reminder of the unpredictability of the future and the potential for individuals to glimpse beyond the present into what lies ahead. For sceptics, it serves as a cautionary tale about the dangers of retrofitting and the human tendency to find patterns in even the most ambiguous predictions.

Conclusion: 9/11 and the Power of Prophecy

Baba Vanga's alleged prediction of the 9/11 attacks remains one of the most discussed and debated aspects of her legacy. Whether viewed as a remarkable example of her prophetic abilities or as a case of retroactive interpretation, the prophecy continues to captivate the imagination. It highlights the enduring human fascination with prophecy, the desire to make sense of world events, and the ways in which symbolic language can shape our understanding of the future.

In this chapter, we explore how Baba Vanga's 9/11 prophecy has become a symbol of her broader legacy as a mystic, seer, and prophet. While the truth of her foresight remains open to debate, there is no denying the profound impact of this prophecy on those who believe in her vision—and on the continuing mystery surrounding the power of prophecy itself.

The 2004 Tsunami: Nature's Fury Foretold

On December 26, 2004, a devastating tsunami struck the Indian Ocean region, triggered by a massive undersea earthquake off the coast of Sumatra, Indonesia. The resulting waves reached heights of up to 100 feet and caused widespread destruction across 14 countries, including Indonesia, Thailand, Sri Lanka, India, and the Maldives. The death toll was catastrophic, with more than 230,000 people losing their lives. The event remains one of the deadliest natural disasters in recorded history, and its impact is still felt in the affected regions.

Among those who claim to have foreseen this disaster is Baba Vanga, the Bulgarian mystic whose prophecies have captivated millions. According to her followers, Baba Vanga predicted the 2004 tsunami years before it occurred, describing a "great wave" that would sweep across coastlines, bringing death and destruction. This chapter delves into Baba Vanga's alleged prophecy of the 2004 tsunami, the aftermath of the disaster, and the ongoing debate about whether her vision truly foretold one of nature's most destructive events.

Baba Vanga's Vision: The "Great Wave" Prophecy

Baba Vanga's followers often point to a specific prophecy in which she allegedly warned of a "great wave" that would engulf coastal regions and cause unprecedented devastation. According to reports, she described this wave as a natural disaster that would strike suddenly and leave behind massive destruction. The prophecy, they argue, aligns closely with the 2004 tsunami, particularly in its description of the force and scale of the disaster.

Her followers believe that this vision was one of many that predicted environmental disasters, which Baba Vanga frequently spoke about throughout her life. In this particular prophecy, she is said to have mentioned that the wave would hit "southern lands," which some interpret as a reference to the Indian Ocean region. The description of water as a force of destruction fits with the images of the tsunami waves sweeping through villages and cities, wiping out homes, infrastructure, and entire communities.

The timing of her prediction remains unclear, as Baba Vanga's prophecies were often passed down orally and recorded later, making it difficult to pinpoint when exactly she made this specific forecast. Nevertheless, for her followers, the connection between her vision and the events of December 26, 2004, is undeniable.

The Tsunami's Devastation

The 2004 Indian Ocean tsunami was triggered by a magnitude 9.1 earthquake, one of the strongest ever recorded. The quake ruptured a massive section of the seafloor, displacing enormous amounts of water and sending powerful waves across the Indian Ocean. In a matter of hours, these waves reached coastal communities in Indonesia, Thailand, Sri Lanka, India, and beyond, causing widespread destruction and loss of life.

Entire towns and villages were swept away in the tsunami's path. In some areas, the waves reached as far as two miles inland, obliterating everything in their wake. Survivors described the experience as one of sheer terror, with no warning and little chance of escape. The economic and infrastructural damage was immense, and the psychological toll on survivors and families who lost loved ones was profound.

The tsunami also revealed the vulnerability of coastal communities to such natural disasters, particularly in regions with limited resources and preparedness measures. The disaster prompted a global humanitarian response, with countries and organizations around the world providing aid to the affected regions. In the years that followed, efforts were made to improve early warning systems and preparedness for future tsunamis, though the scars left by the disaster would take much longer to heal.

Nature's Fury and Prophecy: Interpretations of the "Great Wave"

Baba Vanga's prophecy of a "great wave" is often viewed as one of her most striking and accurate predictions, especially given the scale and severity of the 2004 tsunami. For her followers, the alignment between her vision and the actual events offers proof of her prophetic abilities. The vividness of the "great wave" imagery, combined with the sheer magnitude of the disaster, makes it difficult for believers to dismiss the prophecy as mere coincidence.

The prophecy also fits within a broader pattern of Baba Vanga's predictions about environmental disasters. She frequently spoke of the forces of nature—earthquakes, floods, storms, and other calamities—as key players in the future of humanity. Her warnings about environmental degradation and climate change are particularly resonant today, as extreme weather events and rising sea levels increasingly dominate global headlines.

However, sceptics remain unconvinced. They argue that the language of the prophecy is too vague to be considered a clear prediction of the 2004 tsunami. The phrase "great wave" could refer to many different types of events, from metaphorical upheavals to other natural disasters like hurricanes or floods. Additionally, Baba Vanga's prophecies were often recorded after the fact, making it difficult to determine whether they were truly made before the event or were later reinterpreted to fit specific occurrences.

The geographical ambiguity of her prophecy also raises questions. While some interpret her reference to "southern lands" as pointing to the Indian Ocean region, others argue that this is too general to be seen as a direct prediction of the specific areas hit by the 2004 tsunami. In their view, the prophecy is an example of retroactive fitting, where a vague statement is matched to an event after it occurs.

Environmental Prophecies and Modern-Day Relevance

Beyond the specific prophecy of the 2004 tsunami, Baba Vanga's warnings about environmental disasters have taken on new relevance in the 21st century. As climate change accelerates, causing rising sea levels, more frequent hurricanes, and unpredictable weather patterns, her visions of nature's fury resonate with a modern audience. The 2004 tsunami, while a tragic example of natural disaster, is part of a broader global conversation about humanity's relationship with the environment.

Her prophecies about environmental degradation align with contemporary concerns about the state of the planet. Scientists have long warned that climate change will lead to more frequent and severe natural disasters, including storms, droughts, wildfires, and floods. The 2004 tsunami, while triggered by a geological event, serves as a stark reminder of how vulnerable coastal communities can be to such forces, and how the impacts of climate-related disasters may become more severe in the future.

In this sense, Baba Vanga's prophecies about nature can be seen not just as predictions but as warnings—calls for humanity to recognize its role in the degradation of the environment and to take action before it's too late. Her vision of the "great wave" may serve as a metaphor for the larger environmental challenges facing the world, challenges that require global cooperation and resilience.

The Ongoing Debate: Truth or Myth?

As with many of Baba Vanga's prophecies, the debate over the accuracy of her prediction regarding the 2004 tsunami remains unresolved. For her believers, the prophecy stands as a clear example of her ability to foresee major world events, particularly those involving natural disasters. The specificity of the "great wave" imagery and its correlation with the devastating tsunami seem too significant to dismiss as coincidence.

On the other hand, sceptics argue that the vagueness of the prophecy and the lack of verifiable records weaken the case for Baba Vanga's accuracy. They view the prophecy as an example of how symbolic language can be applied to various events after the fact, making it more a matter of interpretation than true foresight. This debate is emblematic of the larger questions surrounding Baba Vanga's legacy—was she truly a mystic with the ability to see into the future, or were her predictions a product of cultural myth and post-event reinterpretation?

Conclusion: The Tsunami and the Power of Prophecy

Baba Vanga's alleged prophecy of the 2004 tsunami is one of the most compelling examples of her foresight, combining vivid imagery with a real-world event of immense significance. Whether or not one believes in her prophetic abilities, the connection between her vision of the "great wave" and the actual disaster is a striking reminder of the unpredictability and power of nature.

The 2004 tsunami was a tragic event that reshaped the lives of millions, and Baba Vanga's prophecy, whether true or mythical, continues to resonate in discussions about the fragility of life and the forces beyond human control. In this chapter, we explore how the prophecy has been interpreted, the ongoing debate surrounding its accuracy, and the broader implications of Baba Vanga's warnings about environmental disasters.

As we face new and ongoing environmental challenges in the 21st century, Baba Vanga's vision of the "great wave" serves as both a symbol of nature's fury and a reminder of humanity's responsibility to safeguard the planet for future generations.

Presidential Visions: Obama, Trump, and Vanga's Political Prophecies

Baba Vanga's prophecies about political figures and world events have garnered significant attention, particularly those related to the presidencies of Barack Obama and Donald Trump. Although she passed away in 1996, long before either man came to power, her alleged predictions about these two influential figures have captivated believers and sparked debate. In this chapter, we delve into Baba Vanga's political prophecies regarding Obama, Trump, and other leaders, exploring how these visions align—or don't—with the events that unfolded during their presidencies.

Barack Obama: The First Black President

One of Baba Vanga's most celebrated political prophecies is her alleged prediction of the election of the first African American president of the United States. According to some accounts, she foresaw that the 44th president of the United States would be a person of African descent, a prediction that seemed to come true with the election of Barack Obama in 2008. His rise to the presidency was a historic moment, breaking racial barriers in the highest office of the United States.

In the context of Baba Vanga's broader prophecies, the prediction of Obama's presidency is seen as a significant validation of her abilities. At the time she made this prediction, the idea of an African American president seemed far-fetched to many, given the racial tensions and inequalities that still persisted in the United States. Obama's election was a moment of profound change, both in terms of race relations and the shifting political landscape in America.

However, the prophecy did not end with Obama's election. Baba Vanga is also said to have predicted that this African American president would face enormous challenges and that his presidency would be marked by a period of severe crisis. Some of her followers believe that this refers to the economic downturn of 2008, which led to the Great Recession, as well as the political and racial tensions that continued to dominate Obama's time in office. The struggles he faced, including a divided Congress and opposition to his policies like the Affordable Care Act, are seen by believers as evidence of Baba Vanga's foresight.

While sceptics argue that predicting the eventual election of a black president was a reasonable assumption given the civil rights advancements in the United States, Baba Vanga's followers maintain that the accuracy of this prophecy lies not just in Obama's election but in the challenges and crises that marked his presidency.

Donald Trump: The Chaos President

Baba Vanga's followers also point to her prophecies in connection with Donald Trump's presidency, which they believe she predicted as a time of great chaos and instability. According to some interpretations of her visions, she foresaw a divisive and controversial leader who would emerge in the United States, disrupting the political and social order. Trump, with his unconventional approach to politics, his polarizing rhetoric, and the significant upheaval during his term, seemed to fit this description for many of her followers.

One of the most notable aspects of Trump's presidency was the deep division it caused in the American political landscape. His presidency saw intense political polarization, protests, investigations, and a global pandemic that further strained the fabric of American society. From the impeachment proceedings to the controversy surrounding his handling of COVID-19, Trump's tenure was marked by constant turmoil, which some interpret as aligning with Baba Vanga's predictions of a "leader bringing chaos."

In addition to domestic challenges, Trump's presidency had significant global implications. Baba Vanga's prophecy that the United States would face an economic crisis under this leader is often linked to the trade wars initiated by Trump, particularly with China, as well as the impact of the COVID-19 pandemic on the global economy. Although Trump's supporters argue that his presidency brought economic growth prior to the pandemic, others see his administration as a period of economic uncertainty and global instability.

Sceptics, however, argue that the connection between Baba Vanga's prophecy and Trump's presidency is tenuous at best. They claim that describing any future political leader as "chaotic" or "controversial" could apply to a wide range of figures, especially in a country as politically dynamic as the United States. The broad language of the prophecy, they argue, allows for a wide range of interpretations, making it easy to retroactively apply to Trump's presidency.

Other Political Prophecies: Global Leaders and Upheavals

Beyond Obama and Trump, Baba Vanga's prophecies also touched on the global political landscape, including predictions of significant upheavals in Europe, Russia, and the Middle East. She reportedly foresaw the collapse of the Soviet Union, the reunification of East and West Germany, and the breakup of Yugoslavia—predictions that came true in the late 20th century. Her prophecies about the resurgence of Russia as a global power, under a strong leader, are often linked to Vladimir Putin's rise and the increasing influence of Russia on the world stage.

Baba Vanga is also said to have predicted conflicts and revolutions across the Middle East, which some interpret as a reference to the Arab Spring, the Syrian civil war, and the rise of ISIS. Her visions of political instability in these regions, combined with her warnings about terrorism and extremism, seem to mirror the crises that have unfolded over the past two decades. For her followers, these predictions further solidify her reputation as a prophet capable of foreseeing major world events long before they occurred.

However, as with her predictions regarding Obama and Trump, sceptics point out the difficulty of verifying the accuracy of these prophecies. Much of what is attributed to Baba Vanga was passed down orally, and specific details about when and how she made these predictions are often lacking. Critics argue that many of her political prophecies are vague and can be interpreted to fit various events after the fact, making it difficult to determine whether they were truly predictive or simply coincidences.

Interpreting Political Prophecies: The Role of Symbolism and Context

One of the challenges in assessing Baba Vanga's political prophecies, particularly those involving Obama and Trump, is the use of symbolic language and broad themes. Prophecies about political leaders often include references to chaos, crises, and challenges, all of which can be interpreted in various ways depending on the context. In the case of Obama, for example, the prophecy of a "great crisis" could refer to the economic recession, political gridlock, or racial tensions that marked his presidency. Similarly, the prediction of a "chaotic leader" could be applied to many political figures throughout history, not just Trump.

Symbolism plays a significant role in how Baba Vanga's prophecies are understood. Her use of metaphorical language, such as describing leaders as "figures of darkness" or foreseeing "waves of unrest," allows for flexible interpretation, which can be both a strength and a weakness of her predictions. For her followers, these symbolic descriptions are part of what makes her prophecies so powerful, as they capture the essence of political events without being constrained by specific details. For sceptics, however, this lack of specificity makes it easier to apply the prophecies retroactively to various events.

The Power of Political Prophecies: Belief, Influence, and Legacy

Whether or not one believes in the accuracy of Baba Vanga's political prophecies, there is no denying the impact they have had on her legacy. Her predictions about world leaders, including Obama and Trump, reflect the public's fascination with politics and the desire to make sense of global events. Prophecies, by their nature, offer a sense of order in a chaotic world, giving people a framework to understand the unpredictable and often tumultuous nature of political power.

Baba Vanga's influence extends beyond her specific predictions; she has become a cultural figure whose visions are referenced in discussions about world events, especially in times of political uncertainty. Her reputation as a mystic capable of foreseeing both triumphs and disasters allows her prophecies to remain relevant, even as new leaders emerge and new challenges arise. The connection between her political predictions and real-world events, whether interpreted as truth or myth, continues to captivate those who seek to understand the deeper forces shaping our world.

Baba Vanga's alleged prophecies about the presidencies of Barack Obama and Donald Trump offer a unique lens through which to view the intersection of mysticism and modern politics. Her predictions, whether seen as accurate foresight or symbolic interpretations, reflect broader themes of crisis, leadership, and change—issues that continue to dominate the political landscape today. In this chapter, we have explored how Baba Vanga's followers interpret her visions of Obama and Trump, as well as the challenges posed by the symbolic and sometimes ambiguous nature of her prophecies. Whether her political predictions are viewed as divine insight or cultural myth, they remain a fascinating part of her legacy, offering both warnings and reflections on the ever-changing world of politics. As we continue to witness new political developments and global transformations, Baba Vanga's visions will likely continue to spark debate, intrigue, and inspiration.

Solar Storms and Space: Baba Vanga's Celestial Predictions

Baba Vanga's prophecies were not limited to earthly matters such as politics, natural disasters, and social upheavals; she also made several predictions regarding celestial events and humanity's relationship with space. Among her most fascinating and far-reaching visions were those concerning solar storms, space exploration, and humanity's future beyond Earth. These celestial predictions reflect a broader understanding of the universe's powerful and unpredictable forces, as well as humanity's desire to explore and harness the cosmos.

In this chapter, we delve into Baba Vanga's predictions related to space, focusing on her warnings about solar storms and their potential to disrupt life on Earth, as well as her prophecies regarding the future of space exploration and humanity's journey into the cosmos. We will explore the scientific basis behind some of these predictions, the cultural fascination with space prophecy, and the ongoing debates about the accuracy and relevance of her celestial visions.

Solar Storms: The Power of the Sun Unleashed

One of Baba Vanga's most striking celestial prophecies involves solar storms—massive eruptions of energy from the Sun that have the potential to cause widespread damage on Earth. She reportedly foresaw that a powerful solar storm would strike the planet in the 21st century, causing catastrophic disruptions to technology and communications. According to her followers, this event would have far-reaching consequences, from power grid failures to communication blackouts, and could plunge parts of the world into chaos.

Solar storms, or coronal mass ejections (CMEs), occur when the Sun releases a large amount of solar plasma and electromagnetic radiation into space. If these solar particles collide with Earth's magnetosphere, they can cause geomagnetic storms, which may disrupt satellite operations, power grids, and radio communications. While solar storms are a natural part of the Sun's activity cycle, particularly during periods of increased solar flare activity known as solar maximums, a particularly large or severe storm could have significant consequences.

Baba Vanga's prophecy of a devastating solar storm aligns with real-world scientific concerns. In recent years, scientists and space weather experts have warned about the potential dangers posed by solar storms, particularly as our reliance on satellite technology, digital communications, and power grids has increased. A powerful geomagnetic storm could disrupt modern life in ways that were unthinkable in earlier centuries, potentially causing economic and social chaos.

One of the most famous examples of a solar storm's impact occurred in 1859, during the so-called Carrington Event, when a massive solar flare caused widespread disruptions to telegraph systems and produced spectacular auroras visible as far south as the Caribbean. While society in 1859 was less reliant on technology than today, a similar event in the modern era could have far more severe consequences.

For Baba Vanga's followers, her prophecy of a solar storm serves as a warning about humanity's vulnerability to the forces of the universe. The Sun, which provides life-sustaining energy, also possesses the power to disrupt and destroy, a duality reflected in many of her other environmental and cosmic predictions. The potential for a solar storm to cause widespread devastation underscores the fragility of modern civilization and its dependence on technology.

Space Exploration: Humanity's Future Among the Stars

In addition to her warnings about solar storms, Baba Vanga also made several prophecies regarding humanity's future in space. She reportedly foresaw that by the early 21st century, humans would begin serious efforts to colonize other planets and explore distant parts of the solar system. In her vision, space exploration would become one of humanity's most important endeavors, driven by a combination of necessity and curiosity.

This prophecy has resonated with many, particularly as space exploration has gained renewed attention in recent years. With private companies like SpaceX pushing the boundaries of space travel and government agencies like NASA planning missions to Mars, the idea of humans living on other planets no longer seems confined to science fiction. Baba Vanga's prediction of space colonization is increasingly plausible as advances in technology, space engineering, and life support systems bring us closer to achieving this goal.

In her prophecy, Baba Vanga foresaw that humans would initially explore Mars as a potential backup for life on Earth, a vision that aligns with modern plans for Mars exploration and colonization. SpaceX founder Elon Musk, for example, has long advocated for the colonization of Mars as a "plan B" in case of catastrophic events on Earth, such as nuclear war, environmental collapse, or an asteroid impact. Baba Vanga's followers believe her vision of humans settling on Mars reflects a growing recognition of the need to explore space for the long-term survival of the human race.

However, Baba Vanga's vision of space exploration did not come without warnings. She predicted that humanity's attempts to colonize other planets would be fraught with challenges and dangers, including conflicts with other civilizations. As discussed in her prophecy regarding the war on Mars in 3005, she foresaw that space exploration would bring humans into contact with extraterrestrial life, potentially leading to conflicts over resources and territory. This vision serves as both a hopeful and cautionary tale—while space offers a new frontier for human achievement, it also presents unknown risks and threats.

The Search for Extraterrestrial Life

Another of Baba Vanga's celestial prophecies involves the discovery of extraterrestrial life, which she believed would occur by the 22nd century. According to her vision, humans would make contact with an advanced alien civilization, and this discovery would fundamentally change humanity's understanding of its place in the universe. This theme of contact with extraterrestrial beings is central to many of her space-related predictions, and she foresaw that such an encounter would bring both scientific advancement and existential questions.

The search for extraterrestrial life has long fascinated scientists and the general public alike. With the discovery of potentially habitable exoplanets, the detection of strange signals from space, and ongoing missions to Mars and other planets, the possibility of finding life beyond Earth has never seemed more real. Baba Vanga's prophecy taps into this collective curiosity, suggesting that humanity's journey into space will eventually lead to the discovery of intelligent life forms.

In her vision, the discovery of extraterrestrial life would have profound spiritual, scientific, and social implications. It would challenge long-held beliefs about humanity's uniqueness and could inspire a new era of cooperation and collaboration between species. However, Baba Vanga also warned that this discovery could lead to conflict, as humans and aliens vie for resources or struggle to understand each other's intentions.

For her followers, Baba Vanga's prophecy of extraterrestrial contact is both an exciting and daunting prospect. It speaks to humanity's enduring desire to explore the unknown, but also serves as a reminder that the universe is vast and filled with forces and entities beyond our comprehension. Whether this prophecy will come true remains to be seen, but the search for life in the cosmos continues to be one of the most compelling scientific pursuits of the modern age.

Interpreting Celestial Prophecies: Symbolism and Science

As with many of Baba Vanga's prophecies, the celestial predictions about solar storms, space exploration, and extraterrestrial contact are often interpreted through both a symbolic and scientific lens. Her warnings about solar storms, for example, may be seen as metaphors for the fragility of human life and civilization in the face of cosmic forces. The Sun, while providing life, also holds the power to destroy, a duality that speaks to the larger theme of humanity's vulnerability to the universe's unpredictable forces.

Similarly, her prophecies about space exploration and alien contact reflect both a literal prediction of humanity's future endeavors and a symbolic exploration of humanity's quest for knowledge. Space, in this context, represents the ultimate frontier—a place of discovery, risk, and transformation. Baba Vanga's visions of humans venturing into space and encountering other civilizations can be seen as metaphors for humanity's ongoing search for meaning and its desire to transcend the limits of Earth.

The scientific basis for some of Baba Vanga's celestial predictions adds to their intrigue. Solar storms, the colonization of Mars, and the search for extraterrestrial life are all real-world topics of significant scientific interest, and her followers argue that her ability to foresee these developments is evidence of her prophetic insight. Sceptics, however, point out that many of these themes are common in both scientific discourse and science fiction, making it difficult to assess whether her predictions were truly unique or simply reflective of broader cultural ideas.

CONCLUSION: THE MYSTERIES of the Cosmos and Baba Vanga's Legacy

Baba Vanga's celestial predictions offer a fascinating glimpse into her broader vision of the universe and humanity's place within it. Whether warning of solar storms that could disrupt life on Earth or foreseeing the colonization of distant planets, her prophecies capture both the potential and peril of humanity's relationship with the cosmos. Her vision of space exploration as a defining feature of humanity's future resonates with the scientific advancements of today, while her warnings about the dangers of space serve as a reminder that the universe remains an unpredictable and powerful force.

In this chapter, we explore Baba Vanga's celestial predictions, from the looming threat of solar storms to the promise of extraterrestrial contact. While some of her prophecies align with scientific understanding, others remain open to interpretation, reflecting the complex interplay between mysticism, symbolism, and science. As humanity continues to reach for the stars, Baba Vanga's visions of space and the cosmos will likely remain a source of both intrigue and debate, offering a mystical perspective on the challenges and opportunities that lie beyond our planet.

The Changing Earth Orbit: Baba Vanga's Environmental Forecasts

Among Baba Vanga's many prophecies, her predictions regarding environmental changes and their potential catastrophic effects on the Earth stand out as some of her most foreboding warnings. One of her most alarming visions concerned the Earth's orbit itself, foreseeing a time when the planet's orbit would shift, leading to massive environmental upheaval and far-reaching consequences for humanity. This prediction, along with her other environmental forecasts, aligns with the growing concerns about climate change, the fragility of Earth's ecosystems, and humanity's impact on the natural world.

In this chapter, we will explore Baba Vanga's prediction about the changing orbit of Earth, its potential implications, and how her environmental prophecies connect with the modern scientific understanding of climate change, ecological degradation, and humanity's struggle to adapt to a rapidly changing planet. Her visions serve as both a warning and a reflection on the precarious balance between nature and human civilization.

The Prophecy: Earth's Orbit Shift

One of Baba Vanga's most unsettling environmental predictions involved a dramatic shift in Earth's orbit, which she foresaw occurring sometime in the 21st century. According to her prophecy, this shift would disrupt the planet's climate and ecosystems, causing extreme weather events, rising sea levels, and widespread environmental destruction. The result would be a period of chaos as humanity struggled to cope with the changing conditions and the devastating impact on agriculture, water resources, and coastal communities.

The idea of Earth's orbit shifting may seem far-fetched, but in fact, the planet's orbit does naturally change over long periods of time due to gravitational forces exerted by other celestial bodies, particularly the Moon and the Sun, as well as the gravitational pull of other planets. These changes are part of a process known as *orbital variations*, or *Milankovitch cycles*, which affect the distribution of solar energy on Earth and have been linked to past ice ages and periods of warming.

However, the type of sudden, dramatic orbital shift Baba Vanga described would be far beyond the gradual changes seen in Milankovitch cycles. In her vision, the shift is a catastrophic event, leading to immediate and severe environmental consequences. Such a scenario could theoretically be caused by an external force, such as a massive asteroid impact or another cosmic event, though no such threats are currently known to be imminent. The scientific community generally considers Earth's orbit to be relatively stable over short timescales, but the idea of a shift resonates as a metaphor for the broader environmental instability humanity faces today.

Environmental Impacts of an Orbital Shift

If Earth's orbit were to change significantly, the effects on the planet would be profound. A shift in the distance between Earth and the Sun would alter the amount of solar radiation reaching the surface, disrupting the delicate balance that maintains the planet's climate. This could lead to extreme changes in temperature, potentially plunging some regions into severe cold while others experience unbearable heat. Such disruptions would have a cascading effect on global weather patterns, ocean currents, and ecosystems.

One of the most immediate consequences of an orbital shift would be its impact on agriculture and food production. Crops depend on relatively stable weather patterns and temperatures, and even small changes can dramatically reduce yields. A significant shift in Earth's orbit could render large areas of land uninhabitable or unsuitable for farming, leading to widespread food shortages and famine. Water resources would also be affected, as changes in precipitation patterns and the melting of ice caps would alter the availability of freshwater in many regions.

Coastal communities would be particularly vulnerable to the effects of an orbital shift. Rising sea levels, already a concern due to climate change, could accelerate dramatically if the planet's temperature increased, causing polar ice caps to melt at an unprecedented rate. Baba Vanga's prophecy of coastal destruction aligns with current concerns about the vulnerability of coastal cities to flooding and storm surges, particularly as sea levels rise due to global warming.

In her vision, the orbital shift also leads to more frequent and severe natural disasters, including hurricanes, droughts, and wildfires. These disasters, combined with the economic and social disruption caused by the environmental changes, would push humanity to the brink of collapse, testing the resilience of societies around the world. For Baba Vanga's followers, this prophecy serves as a warning about the dangers of ignoring the signs of environmental degradation and the urgent need to address the root causes of climate instability.

Climate Change and Modern Environmental Challenges

While the idea of a sudden orbital shift is speculative, Baba Vanga's broader environmental prophecies align closely with modern scientific understanding of climate change and the ecological crises facing the planet today. Climate scientists warn that the Earth is already experiencing significant environmental changes due to human activities, particularly the burning of fossil fuels, deforestation, and industrial pollution. These activities have led to a rapid increase in greenhouse gas concentrations, which trap heat in the atmosphere and drive global warming.

The effects of climate change are already being felt around the world, with rising temperatures, shifting weather patterns, and an increase in the frequency and intensity of extreme weather events. Wildfires, droughts, floods, and storms are becoming more common, and the consequences for ecosystems and human societies are becoming increasingly severe. These developments echo Baba Vanga's warnings about environmental collapse and the challenges humanity will face in adapting to these changes.

In many ways, Baba Vanga's prophecy about the changing Earth orbit can be interpreted as a metaphor for the broader environmental upheavals already underway. While a literal shift in the planet's orbit may not be imminent, the destabilization of Earth's climate due to human actions is a real and pressing concern. The planetary systems that support life are interconnected, and as they become destabilized, the impacts ripple across ecosystems, economies, and communities.

Humanity's Response to Environmental Change

One of the central themes of Baba Vanga's environmental prophecies is the idea that humanity will be forced to confront its impact on the planet and find ways to adapt to the changing environment. In her vision, the orbital shift and subsequent environmental collapse serve as a wake-up call, pushing humanity to develop new technologies and strategies to mitigate the damage and survive in a transformed world.

This theme resonates with current discussions about climate adaptation and mitigation. As the effects of climate change become more pronounced, governments, scientists, and communities around the world are grappling with how to respond. Efforts to reduce greenhouse gas emissions through renewable energy, carbon capture technologies, and reforestation are critical components of the fight against climate change, but they may not be enough to prevent some of the worst impacts.

At the same time, adaptation strategies—such as building more resilient infrastructure, developing drought-resistant crops, and improving disaster preparedness—are becoming increasingly important. In many ways, Baba Vanga's prophecy can be seen as a call to action, urging humanity to recognize the urgency of the environmental crisis and take bold steps to address it before it's too late.

The Symbolism of Orbital Shifts: A Metaphor for Human Disruption

Baba Vanga's prophecy about Earth's orbit shifting can also be interpreted symbolically, as a metaphor for the broader disruptions caused by humanity's exploitation of natural resources. The idea of the planet itself being thrown off course reflects the ways in which human activities have destabilized the environment, pushing ecosystems beyond their capacity to recover. Industrialization, urbanization, and deforestation have altered the planet's natural rhythms, leading to the environmental crises we face today.

This interpretation of the prophecy aligns with the view that humanity's relationship with nature is at a tipping point. Just as an orbital shift would disrupt the balance of life on Earth, so too have human actions disrupted the delicate balance that sustains ecosystems and biodiversity. In this sense, Baba Vanga's vision serves as a powerful reminder of the consequences of unchecked environmental degradation and the need for a more harmonious relationship with the natural world.

CONCLUSION: BABA VANGA'S Environmental Legacy

Baba Vanga's prophecy of a changing Earth orbit, while dramatic and speculative, offers a powerful lens through which to explore the broader environmental challenges facing humanity today. Whether interpreted literally or symbolically, her vision of a planet in crisis resonates with modern concerns about climate change, ecological collapse, and the vulnerability of human societies to environmental disruptions.

In this chapter, we explore Baba Vanga's environmental forecasts, from her warnings about a shifting orbit to her broader predictions of climate-related disasters. Her prophecies, while mysterious and open to interpretation, serve as both a cautionary tale and a call to action. As humanity faces the profound challenges of a changing planet, her visions remind us of the urgent need to protect and preserve the Earth's fragile ecosystems.

As we move further into the 21st century, Baba Vanga's environmental prophecies continue to resonate, offering a mystical perspective on the scientific realities of climate change and the pressing need for global action. Whether viewed as a literal prediction or a metaphor for the larger forces at play, her vision of a shifting Earth orbit reflects the precariousness of our planet's future and the importance of recognizing our role in shaping it.

Bioweapons and Humanity's Future Threats

Among Baba Vanga's many chilling prophecies, one that resonates with particular urgency in today's world is her prediction about the development and use of bioweapons—biological agents designed to harm or kill large populations. In her visions, Baba Vanga foresaw a future in which bioweapons would pose an existential threat to humanity, with deadly consequences that could lead to widespread suffering, disease, and global unrest. As the world becomes more interconnected and technological advances continue, the potential for bioweapons to be used as instruments of terror or warfare grows more concerning. This chapter explores Baba Vanga's prophecies regarding bioweapons, the historical context of biological warfare, and the modern-day threats posed by these dangerous agents.

The Prophecy: The Rise of Bioweapons

Baba Vanga reportedly foresaw that in the 21st century, humanity would face the terrifying prospect of bioweapons being unleashed, causing untold suffering and the potential for catastrophic pandemics. In her vision, these weapons would not be conventional tools of war, like nuclear arms or missiles, but invisible agents—viruses, bacteria, and other pathogens—that could spread quickly and uncontrollably. She warned that these biological agents would be used not just in warfare, but also as tools of terror, targeting civilian populations and causing widespread fear and chaos.

This prophecy aligns with the growing concerns about the potential for biological weapons to be developed and deployed in the modern world. Unlike traditional weapons, bioweapons have the unique ability to spread silently and quickly, often undetected until it's too late to contain the damage. Baba Vanga's vision of bioweapons as a future threat reflects both the advancements in biotechnology and the dark possibilities that these developments present.

While bioweapons have been used in the past, the technological advancements of the 21st century, particularly in the fields of genetics and synthetic biology, have raised the stakes considerably. Baba Vanga's prophecy of a world grappling with bioweapons reflects not only the historical dangers of biological warfare but also the contemporary fears that humanity is entering a new era where such threats may become more difficult to prevent and control.

A History of Biological Warfare

Biological warfare—the use of pathogens or toxins as weapons—has a long and troubling history. In ancient times, armies would contaminate enemy water supplies with dead bodies or animal carcasses to spread disease. The medieval practice of catapulting plague-infected corpses into besieged cities is another example of early attempts to weaponize disease. As science and medicine advanced, so too did the understanding of how diseases could be harnessed and used deliberately as tools of war.

DURING WORLD WAR I and World War II, the use of chemical weapons such as mustard gas raised alarms about the potential for even more dangerous biological agents to be used in future conflicts. After the horrors of these wars, the Geneva Protocol of 1925 sought to ban the use of biological and chemical weapons, though it did not prohibit research or development of these agents. The advent of modern biotechnology in the 20th century only heightened concerns about the possibility of creating more effective and deadly biological weapons.

One of the most notorious examples of biological warfare research was the Japanese Unit 731 during World War II, which conducted horrific experiments on humans using pathogens such as plague, cholera, and anthrax. These experiments were intended to develop bioweapons for use in warfare, though much of the research remained secret for decades.

The Cold War era saw both the United States and the Soviet Union engage in bioweapons research, despite international efforts to ban such activities. The Biological Weapons Convention (BWC) of 1972 was a landmark treaty that aimed to prohibit the development, production, and stockpiling of biological weapons. While the treaty was a significant step forward, enforcement has been a challenge, and the threat of bioweapons remains a concern to this day.

Modern Threats: Biotechnology and the Weaponization of Disease

In Baba Vanga's prophecy, the future use of bioweapons is depicted as a far more sophisticated and dangerous phenomenon than the crude attempts of the past. With advances in biotechnology, genetic engineering, and synthetic biology, the potential to create tailor-made pathogens that target specific populations, immune systems, or even individuals has become a real possibility. Baba Vanga foresaw the use of these technologies to create deadly viruses and bacteria that could be unleashed as acts of war or terrorism.

Today, the tools to manipulate pathogens at the genetic level are widely available in laboratories around the world, raising concerns about how these technologies could be used for harmful purposes. CRISPR gene-editing technology, for instance, allows scientists to modify DNA with unprecedented precision, which could be used to create bioweapons that are resistant to existing treatments or designed to evade immune responses. While these technologies hold incredible potential for medical advancements, they also represent a significant security threat if used maliciously.

Baba Vanga's vision of bioweapons as invisible threats aligns with modern-day concerns about the difficulty of detecting and preventing biological attacks. Unlike conventional weapons, bioweapons can be deployed covertly, and their effects may not be immediately apparent. In the case of a virus or bacteria, an outbreak could spread for days or weeks before authorities even realize that an attack has occurred, by which time the damage could be extensive.

THE POTENTIAL FOR BIOWEAPONS to cause widespread fear and destabilization is another theme in Baba Vanga's prophecy. In today's interconnected world, a biological attack in one country could quickly spread across borders, leading to global panic, economic collapse, and massive loss of life. The COVID-19 pandemic, though naturally occurring, has demonstrated how quickly a pathogen can spread in a globalized society and how difficult it can be to contain. Baba Vanga's warnings about bioweapons reflect the fear that such a scenario could be intentionally engineered in the future.

Global Terrorism and the Bioweapons Threat

One of the most alarming aspects of Baba Vanga's prophecy is her suggestion that bioweapons could be used by non-state actors, such as terrorist groups, to inflict mass casualties and cause societal collapse. While the use of biological weapons in traditional warfare has been limited due to international agreements, the rise of global terrorism presents a new challenge. Terrorist groups, particularly those motivated by ideological or apocalyptic visions, may seek to use bioweapons to achieve their goals of creating chaos and instilling fear.

The accessibility of biotechnological tools has made it easier for non-state actors to potentially acquire or develop bioweapons. With the right knowledge and equipment, a small group of individuals could theoretically engineer a deadly pathogen and release it in a public space, causing an outbreak with catastrophic consequences. Baba Vanga's prophecy of bioweapons being used to terrorize civilian populations speaks to this modern-day threat and the difficulty of preventing such attacks in an era where technological capabilities are rapidly advancing.

Governments and international organizations have recognized the bioweapons threat, and efforts to strengthen biosecurity measures have been ongoing. The Biological Weapons Convention, for example, has been reinforced with new protocols and monitoring systems aimed at preventing the development and use of bioweapons. However, challenges remain, particularly in ensuring that all nations comply with the treaty and in detecting covert bioweapons programs.

Humanity's Response: Preparing for Future Biological Threats

In Baba Vanga's vision, the future of humanity is closely tied to how well we prepare for and respond to the threats posed by bioweapons. She foresaw that humanity's ability to develop countermeasures—such as vaccines, treatments, and early detection systems—would be crucial in mitigating the damage caused by biological attacks. This prediction aligns with modern efforts to strengthen global health systems and improve preparedness for biological emergencies.

The development of vaccines, antibiotics, and antiviral treatments has been one of the most important tools in combating infectious diseases. In the context of bioweapons, having the ability to rapidly produce and distribute medical countermeasures is critical to limiting the spread of a biological agent. Baba Vanga's prophecy underscores the importance of investing in medical research and ensuring that global health systems are equipped to handle both natural and man-made biological threats.

Another key aspect of preparing for future bioweapons threats is the establishment of robust surveillance and early warning systems. The ability to quickly detect and contain an outbreak, whether natural or intentional, is crucial in preventing widespread casualties. Baba Vanga's warnings about the invisible nature of bioweapons highlight the need for enhanced detection capabilities, including genomic sequencing technologies that can identify new pathogens in real time.

Conclusion: Bioweapons and the Future of Global Security

Baba Vanga's prophecy of bioweapons as a future threat serves as a stark reminder of the dangers posed by biological agents in the 21st century. As advances in biotechnology continue, the potential for these tools to be used for harmful purposes grows, raising urgent questions about how to prevent the development and use of bioweapons. Her vision reflects both the promise and peril of modern science—while biotechnology has the potential to revolutionize medicine and improve human health, it also opens the door to new forms of warfare and terrorism.

In this chapter, we explore Baba Vanga's prophecy of bioweapons and humanity's future threats, drawing connections between her warnings and the real-world challenges facing global security today. Her vision of invisible agents wreaking havoc on civilian populations resonates with contemporary fears about biological warfare and terrorism. As humanity grapples with these threats, Baba Vanga's prophecy serves as both a cautionary tale and a call to action, urging us to be vigilant in safeguarding against the dangers posed by bioweapons.

The future of global security depends on our ability to adapt to the evolving landscape of biological threats. Baba Vanga's prophecy highlights the importance of preparedness, cooperation, and innovation in facing these challenges head-on. Whether or not her vision comes to pass, the warnings about bioweapons remind us that humanity's greatest vulnerabilities often lie in the invisible forces that shape our world.

The Assassination of 2024: A Prophetic Warning

Baba Vanga's prophecy regarding an assassination in 2024 stands out as one of her most ominous predictions for the near future. In this vision, she foresaw the assassination of a prominent global figure, an event that would send shockwaves across the world and trigger significant political and social unrest. For her followers, this prophecy carries a grave warning about the potential for political instability and the ripple effects such an assassination could have on international relations, economic stability, and even global security.

In this chapter, we explore Baba Vanga's prediction of the 2024 assassination, its possible interpretations, and the broader historical and political context surrounding assassinations of influential figures. We also examine the potential implications of such an event and how it could align with or deviate from Baba Vanga's overall vision of the future.

The Prophecy: A High-Profile Assassination

Baba Vanga's prophecy of the 2024 assassination is typically described in vague but troubling terms. She allegedly foresaw that a well-known political leader or figure of great influence would be assassinated in 2024, an event that would destabilize not only the nation where it occurs but also have a far-reaching impact on global affairs. While she did not provide specific details—such as the identity of the figure or the circumstances surrounding the assassination—her vision emphasized the shock and disruption that this event would cause, leading to political chaos and perhaps even conflict.

The idea of a high-profile assassination immediately brings to mind historical events that have had similar repercussions, such as the assassination of Archduke Franz Ferdinand of Austria in 1914, which is widely regarded as the catalyst for World War I, or the assassination of President John F. Kennedy in 1963, which sent the United States into a period of mourning and speculation about the direction of its future. Baba Vanga's prophecy hints at a comparable event in 2024—one that could mark a turning point in modern history.

For her followers, this prophecy serves as a warning of potential instability and the fragility of political structures in a time of increasing division and uncertainty. Whether the assassination will occur in a Western democracy, a rising power, or another part of the world is unclear, but the potential for destabilization and unrest is a common theme in interpretations of this prophecy.

The Historical Impact of Assassinations

Throughout history, the assassination of prominent figures has often led to significant political and social change, sometimes even altering the course of history. These acts of violence, whether politically motivated or carried out by lone individuals, have a profound psychological and emotional impact on societies. Baba Vanga's prophecy of a 2024 assassination calls to mind several historical events where the death of a leader sparked unrest, conflict, or profound societal shifts.

Archduke Franz Ferdinand (1914): The assassination of Archduke Franz Ferdinand of Austria by a Serbian nationalist in 1914 is often cited as the immediate cause of World War I. What was initially a regional crisis quickly escalated into a global conflict as alliances between nations drew them into the war. Baba Vanga's prophecy suggests that the 2024 assassination could have similarly far-reaching consequences, potentially triggering a conflict or political upheaval on a global scale.

John F. Kennedy (1963): The assassination of U.S. President John F. Kennedy in 1963 was a defining moment in American history, plunging the nation into a period of mourning and reflection. The circumstances surrounding Kennedy's assassination led to numerous conspiracy theories, political uncertainty, and a shift in American politics. Similarly, Baba Vanga's prophecy implies that the 2024 assassination could lead to widespread speculation, conspiracy theories, and shifts in power structures.

Martin Luther King Jr. (1968): The assassination of civil rights leader Martin Luther King Jr. in 1968 had a profound impact on the United States, sparking riots in cities across the country and intensifying the civil rights movement. King's death highlighted the deep divisions within American society and the ongoing struggle for racial justice. Baba Vanga's prophecy may suggest that the 2024 assassination will similarly expose societal divisions and fuel existing tensions, leading to unrest.

These historical examples underscore the potential for an assassination to disrupt not only political systems but also social cohesion, as Baba Vanga's followers believe her vision foretells for 2024.

Political Instability and Global Repercussions

Baba Vanga's prophecy of a high-profile assassination in 2024 is often interpreted as a warning of political instability. In an era marked by increasing polarization, nationalism, and geopolitical tensions, the assassination of a prominent leader could act as a tipping point, unleashing a wave of instability that could spread beyond national borders.

One possible scenario is that the assassination could lead to a power vacuum in a politically unstable country, allowing factions to vie for control and creating the conditions for civil war or widespread conflict. Alternatively, if the assassination occurs in a more stable country, it could still provoke massive protests, violent clashes, and a loss of confidence in the government's ability to maintain order.

In a globalized world, the impact of such an event would not be confined to one country. Economic markets could react with volatility, diplomatic relations could be strained, and international organizations might struggle to respond to the crisis. Baba Vanga's followers often interpret this prophecy as a call for vigilance, emphasizing the interconnected nature of modern political systems and the potential for a single event to trigger widespread instability.

Speculation and Potential Targets

Given the lack of specific details in Baba Vanga's prophecy, speculation about who the target of the 2024 assassination might be runs rampant among her followers and interpreters. Some suggest that the prophecy could refer to a world leader such as a president, prime minister, or monarch, whose death would have immediate global implications.

Others speculate that the target could be a leading figure in international finance, technology, or diplomacy—someone whose influence extends beyond their home country and whose assassination would have ripple effects throughout the world.

It is also possible that the target of the assassination could be a figure not currently in power but set to rise in prominence before 2024. Given Baba Vanga's symbolic and often cryptic language, the prophecy may not refer to a political leader at all but to a prominent cultural or religious figure whose death could provoke widespread unrest or division.

Regardless of the specific target, Baba Vanga's prophecy suggests that the assassination will be an unexpected and disruptive event, one that will catch the world off guard and lead to significant consequences.

Interpretations and Skepticism

As with many of Baba Vanga's prophecies, there is considerable debate over the accuracy and meaning of her vision of the 2024 assassination. Some of her followers interpret the prophecy literally, believing that it foretells the actual assassination of a high-profile figure, while others see it as a metaphor for a broader societal collapse or the "assassination" of democratic institutions or freedoms.

Sceptics, however, argue that the prophecy is too vague to be taken seriously, pointing out that assassinations are not uncommon in the modern world, and predicting one is not necessarily a demonstration of prophetic ability. They contend that any prominent figure's assassination could be retroactively linked to Baba Vanga's vision, allowing for flexible interpretations.

Additionally, critics point out that Baba Vanga's prophecies often rely on general themes of chaos, conflict, and upheaval, which can be applied to many different events. While the assassination prophecy is dramatic, they argue that it is no more specific or accurate than her other predictions that have yet to come to pass.

Conclusion: The Assassination of 2024 and Baba Vanga's Legacy

Whether interpreted as a literal warning or a symbolic reflection of deeper societal unrest, Baba Vanga's prophecy of an assassination in 2024 continues to captivate her followers. The idea that a single, violent act could trigger widespread instability and upheaval resonates with contemporary anxieties about the fragility of political systems and the ever-present threat of violence in a polarized world.

In this chapter, we have explored Baba Vanga's prophecy of the 2024 assassination, examining its possible implications and the broader historical and political context of such events. While the truth of her vision remains uncertain, it serves as a reminder of the profound impact that political violence can have on societies and the delicate balance that holds global systems together. As we approach 2024, the prophecy of an assassination remains a source of speculation and concern, particularly for those who believe in Baba Vanga's foresight. Whether or not her prediction comes to pass, it stands as a testament to the enduring power of prophecy to shape our understanding of the future and the ways in which we interpret the world around us.

Economic Crisis on the Horizon: Baba Vanga's Financial Predictions

Baba Vanga's prophecies touched on a wide range of subjects, including political upheavals, natural disasters, and global health crises. However, one of the most striking themes in her visions for the 21st century involves a major economic crisis that she foresaw as being on the horizon. According to Baba Vanga's predictions, this financial disaster would have profound and far-reaching effects, destabilizing economies around the world, leading to widespread unemployment, and causing social unrest.

In this chapter, we explore Baba Vanga's prophecies related to economic crises, examine how these predictions align with current economic trends and concerns, and consider the potential consequences of such a crisis on the global stage. With the interconnectedness of the world's economies, even a localized economic downturn can have ripple effects that impact countries far beyond its origin. Baba Vanga's warnings about financial instability serve as a sobering reminder of the fragility of global markets and the need for vigilance and preparedness.

The Prophecy: A Global Economic Collapse

Baba Vanga's prophecy of an economic crisis warned of a future where the world would face a severe financial downturn, one that would be more destructive and widespread than any previous recession or market crash. According to her vision, this crisis would not be confined to a single country or region but would spread across borders, affecting both developed and developing economies alike. It would bring with it high levels of unemployment, poverty, and civil unrest as governments and institutions struggled to cope with the fallout.

In particular, Baba Vanga foresaw that this financial collapse would be triggered by a combination of factors, including political instability, environmental disasters, and technological disruptions. She predicted that the interconnectedness of the modern world would exacerbate the crisis, with economic problems in one part of the globe quickly spreading to others. As economies faltered, she warned, the gap between the wealthy and the poor would widen, leading to widespread dissatisfaction and protests.

This prophecy resonates with concerns about the global economy's vulnerability to shocks and disruptions. The financial crisis of 2008, which began with the collapse of the housing market in the United States, demonstrated how quickly economic instability could spread across the world. Baba Vanga's prophecy suggests that an even larger and more devastating crisis lies ahead—one that could fundamentally alter the structure of global markets.

Current Economic Trends and Warnings

While Baba Vanga's prophecies remain open to interpretation, many economists and financial experts have expressed concerns about the potential for another major economic downturn in the near future. Several factors have contributed to growing fears of instability in the global economy, including:

Rising Debt Levels: Both government and private sector debt levels have risen dramatically in recent years, particularly in the wake of the COVID-19 pandemic, which forced many countries to take on significant debt to support struggling businesses and citizens. This increased debt burden has led to concerns that countries may be unable to manage future crises without facing insolvency or default.

Inflation and Monetary Policy: In response to the economic fallout from the pandemic, central banks around the world implemented aggressive monetary policies, including lowering interest rates and engaging in massive bond-buying programs. While these measures helped stabilize the economy in the short term, they also contributed to rising inflation. As inflation rates rise, central banks are under pressure to tighten monetary policy, which could slow economic growth and increase the risk of a recession.

Technological Disruptions: Rapid advancements in automation and artificial intelligence are reshaping industries and labor markets around the world. While these technologies hold promise for increased productivity, they also pose significant risks to employment, particularly in sectors where jobs are being replaced by machines. Baba Vanga's prophecy hinted at a future where technology, rather than being a purely beneficial force, could also contribute to economic instability by displacing workers and leading to higher levels of unemployment.

Geopolitical Tensions: Ongoing geopolitical conflicts, such as tensions between major powers like the United States, China, and Russia, as well as regional conflicts in the Middle East and Eastern Europe, have created uncertainty in global markets. Sanctions, trade disputes, and supply chain disruptions add to the potential for economic instability. Baba Vanga's prophecy suggested that political instability would play a key role in triggering the next economic collapse, and these tensions could be seen as precursors to such an event.

Environmental Catastrophes: Baba Vanga's visions often included environmental disasters as triggers for broader crises. In the context of an economic collapse, natural disasters such as hurricanes, wildfires, and floods—many of which are linked to climate change—could exacerbate financial instability by causing damage to infrastructure, disrupting supply chains, and displacing populations.

The Consequences of a Global Economic Crisis

If Baba Vanga's prophecy of a global economic collapse were to come to pass, the consequences could be devastating. Such a crisis would likely lead to significant social and political upheaval, as governments struggle to manage the fallout and maintain stability. Some of the potential consequences include:

Mass Unemployment: One of the most immediate effects of an economic collapse would be a sharp rise in unemployment. As businesses fail and industries contract, millions of people could lose their jobs, leading to widespread poverty and social unrest. Baba Vanga's prophecy suggested that unemployment would be one of the key drivers of the crisis, with entire industries being decimated by technological disruption and economic contraction.

Banking Failures: A global economic collapse could also lead to the failure of major banks and financial institutions, as we saw during the 2008 financial crisis. With governments and central banks unable to provide the necessary support, the financial system could seize up, making it difficult for businesses and consumers to access credit. This, in turn, would deepen the economic downturn and prolong the recovery.

Social Unrest and Protests: Baba Vanga's prophecy hinted at widespread social unrest in the wake of the economic collapse. As inequality worsens and governments struggle to provide for their citizens, protests and riots could break out in countries around the world. This unrest could take many forms, from anti-government demonstrations to violent clashes between different social and political groups.

Collapse of Global Trade: Global trade, which relies on the smooth functioning of international markets and supply chains, would be severely disrupted in the event of a global economic collapse. Countries could become more isolationist, imposing tariffs and restrictions in an attempt to protect their economies. This breakdown in trade would further exacerbate shortages of essential goods, driving up prices and creating economic hardship.

Political Instability and Regime Change: In Baba Vanga's vision, the economic crisis could lead to political instability and the potential for regime change in some countries. Governments that are unable to manage the crisis effectively may face revolts, coups, or other challenges to their authority. In some cases, authoritarian leaders may rise to power as populations demand strong leadership to restore order.

Financial Systems and Preparedness

While Baba Vanga's prophecy paints a bleak picture of the future, governments and international organizations have been working to strengthen financial systems and improve preparedness for future crises. Central banks, such as the U.S. Federal Reserve, the European Central Bank, and the Bank of Japan, have developed tools to manage inflation, support growth, and provide liquidity during times of crisis. Additionally, international bodies like the International Monetary Fund (IMF) and the World Bank play critical roles in providing financial assistance to countries facing economic hardship.

However, the interconnectedness of the global economy means that even the most well-prepared countries are vulnerable to economic shocks originating elsewhere. As we saw during the 2008 financial crisis, events in one part of the world can quickly spiral into a global downturn. Baba Vanga's prophecy serves as a reminder that no country is immune to the effects of a global financial collapse and that continued vigilance and cooperation are essential in preventing such a disaster.

Interpretation and Skepticism

As with many of Baba Vanga's prophecies, interpretations of her vision of a global economic collapse vary. Some of her followers believe that her predictions offer a literal warning about an impending financial disaster, while others see her prophecy as more symbolic, reflecting the deeper systemic issues within the global economy—such as inequality, corruption, and unsustainable growth—that could lead to future crises.

Sceptics, however, argue that predicting an economic crisis is not particularly unique, as financial downturns are a recurring feature of capitalism. They point out that many economists have made similar warnings about the risks posed by rising debt, inflation, and technological disruption. For them, Baba Vanga's prophecy is simply an expression of general concerns about the economy rather than a specific or supernatural prediction.

Conclusion: The Fragility of Global Markets

Baba Vanga's prophecy of an economic crisis serves as both a warning and a reflection of the inherent fragility of global financial systems. In an era of rapid technological change, political instability, and environmental degradation, the risk of a major economic downturn is ever-present. Whether or not her vision comes to pass, the lessons from past crises—such as the Great Depression and the 2008 financial meltdown—underscore the importance of preparedness, cooperation, and vigilance in managing economic instability.

In this chapter, we have explored Baba Vanga's financial predictions and their relevance to current global economic trends. Her prophecy of a global economic collapse highlights the interconnected nature of modern economies and the potential consequences of systemic failures. As governments, businesses, and individuals face an uncertain future, Baba Vanga's vision serves as a reminder of the need to build more resilient, equitable, and sustainable economic systems to withstand the challenges ahead.

The 2012 Phenomenon: Baba Vanga vs. the Mayan Calendar

The year 2012 sparked widespread fascination and fear due to a prophecy stemming from the ancient Mayan calendar, which many believed predicted the end of the world on December 21, 2012. This event, commonly referred to as the "2012 Phenomenon," captivated global attention, as various theories emerged about an impending apocalypse. However, while the Mayan calendar prediction reached fever pitch in popular culture, Baba Vanga's prophecies presented a different perspective on the future.

In this chapter, we will explore the 2012 phenomenon, compare it to Baba Vanga's visions, and examine how both prophecies have been interpreted by believers and sceptics alike. By contrasting the ancient Mayan predictions with Baba Vanga's prophecies, we can gain insight into how societies interpret mystical predictions and their desire to understand—or control—the unknown future.

The Mayan Calendar and the 2012 Prophecy

The foundation of the 2012 phenomenon comes from the Mesoamerican Long Count calendar, created by the ancient Maya civilization. According to the Long Count calendar, the date December 21, 2012, marked the completion of a 5,125-year cycle, leading some to believe that this date signified the end of the world. While Mayan scholars argued that the calendar was never meant to predict an apocalypse, popular interpretations of the date spun wildly out of control.

Many believed that December 21, 2012, would bring about a cataclysmic event, whether it be natural disasters, planetary alignments, or a collision with a rogue planet known as "Nibiru." Speculation about the end of the world fueled books, films, and documentaries, with millions of people anxiously awaiting this prophesied date. The "end of the world" hysteria surrounding 2012 reflected a deep-seated human desire to anticipate and prepare for major world-altering events.

However, in the aftermath of December 21, 2012, when no apocalyptic event occurred, the 2012 phenomenon came to be regarded by many as a misunderstanding of the Mayan calendar or an example of exaggerated interpretations that had taken on a life of their own. Scholars emphasized that the date merely represented the end of one calendar cycle and the beginning of another.

Baba Vanga's Prophecies: No 2012 Apocalypse

Unlike the Mayan calendar's 2012 prediction, Baba Vanga did not foresee an apocalyptic event occurring in 2012. In fact, her prophecies indicated that the world's end would come much later, around the year 5079. While she made several predictions regarding global disasters and challenges—such as environmental catastrophes, conflicts, and economic crises—none of these centered around 2012 as a climactic event for humanity.

FOR BABA VANGA'S FOLLOWERS, this absence of an apocalyptic prediction for 2012 set her apart from other prophetic figures or cultural doomsday theories. Instead, her focus remained on longer-term events that extended far beyond the 2012 phenomenon, portraying human history as a series of struggles, developments, and eventual encounters with cosmic forces. While she foresaw difficult periods ahead, including wars and natural disasters, her vision of humanity's trajectory was more gradual and less focused on an immediate end-of-days scenario.

The Contrast between Baba Vanga and the Mayan Prophecy

While both the Mayan calendar and Baba Vanga's prophecies have captivated the public imagination, they differ significantly in terms of their scope, focus, and cultural impact.

Temporal Focus: The Mayan prophecy was focused on a specific date—December 21, 2012—leading many to believe that a single event would mark the end of the world or the beginning of a new age. Baba Vanga, on the other hand, offered prophecies that spanned centuries, focusing on humanity's long-term future rather than a single apocalyptic moment.

Nature of Predictions: The Mayan prophecy, as it was popularly interpreted, predicted a world-ending event, often accompanied by natural disasters or celestial phenomena. Baba Vanga's prophecies, while foretelling disasters, were more about the ongoing challenges and evolutions humanity would face. Her predictions about future wars, environmental degradation, and technological advancements pointed to a continuous series of trials, rather than a sudden apocalyptic end.

Cultural Context: The Mayan prophecy, rooted in the traditions of an ancient civilization, became a symbol of humanity's enduring fascination with cycles, time, and cosmic influence. Baba Vanga's prophecies, by contrast, are viewed more through the lens of mysticism and modern prophetic traditions. While both offered compelling narratives, the Mayan calendar's cyclical interpretation of time contrasted with Baba Vanga's linear view of the future, which culminated in a distant, but inevitable, end of the world.

Interpretations of the 2012 Phenomenon: A New Age or Apocalyptic Hysteria?

For many believers, the 2012 prophecy was never about a literal end of the world, but rather a symbolic shift in consciousness or a transformation of human society. Some New Age thinkers interpreted the end of the Mayan calendar cycle as the beginning of a new spiritual era—an awakening of human potential, greater unity, and enlightenment. In this interpretation, the end of the cycle did not signify destruction, but renewal.

In contrast, others clung to more dramatic and fear-based interpretations, predicting catastrophic events like solar flares, asteroid impacts, or a pole shift. These doomsday scenarios reflected not only misunderstandings of the Mayan calendar but also modern anxieties about climate change, political instability, and the fragility of human existence.

Baba Vanga's prophecies, while avoiding the hysteria surrounding a specific date, shared some thematic similarities with these New Age interpretations of transformation. Her predictions about environmental collapse, human contact with extraterrestrial civilizations, and technological advancements suggested that humanity would undergo significant changes in the coming centuries, though she saw these shifts as part of a gradual process rather than a sudden event tied to a single year.

Aftermath of 2012: Reassessing Prophecy and the Human Desire for Answers

When December 21, 2012, passed without incident, many people began to reassess the 2012 prophecy and the broader idea of doomsday predictions. The failure of the apocalypse to materialize prompted a shift in public perception about prophecy and the way such predictions are interpreted and shared.

For some, the 2012 phenomenon became a cautionary tale about the dangers of apocalyptic thinking and the human tendency to seek definitive answers about the future. It also underscored how easily predictions can be misinterpreted or manipulated to fit contemporary fears and concerns. The 2012 prophecy, like many others throughout history, ultimately reflected the deep uncertainty that people feel about the future and the desire for control over the unknown.

In contrast, Baba Vanga's long-term prophecies, while still open to interpretation, did not carry the same level of specific time-bound fear. Her focus on distant events such as alien contact in 2130, the colonization of Mars in 3005, and the end of the world in 5079 allowed her followers to focus more on the broader trajectory of humanity's evolution rather than an immediate catastrophe.

Conclusion: Prophecies and Human Nature

The 2012 phenomenon and Baba Vanga's prophecies both illustrate the timeless human fascination with predicting the future and the powerful role prophecy plays in shaping societal beliefs. Whether through ancient calendars or modern mystics, humanity's desire to understand the course of time and anticipate major events speaks to our innate curiosity and our fears about what lies ahead.

In this chapter, we explored the dramatic contrast between the Mayan calendar's 2012 prediction and Baba Vanga's more extended visions of the future. While the former captivated global attention with its fixed date and apocalyptic imagery, the latter provided a broader, more nuanced view of humanity's future, marked by gradual changes, challenges, and ultimately, an eventual end far in the future.

Baba Vanga's prophecies, free from the hysteria of specific doomsday dates, continue to resonate with her followers, offering both warnings and hope as humanity moves forward. The lessons of 2012 serve as a reminder that while prophecy may provide insight or caution, it is ultimately our actions in the present that shape the future we experience.

Believers and Sceptics: Baba Vanga's Followers and Critics

Baba Vanga, the blind Bulgarian mystic, has become a polarizing figure, inspiring deep devotion among her followers and intense skepticism from her critics. Her reputation as a prophet stems from her numerous predictions, which range from global events like natural disasters and political upheavals to more personal insights into people's lives. Over the years, her visions have been credited with foreseeing major world events, including the 9/11 terrorist attacks and the rise of ISIS, while others view her prophecies as vague or coincidental at best.

In this chapter, we explore the divide between Baba Vanga's believers and her sceptics, examining the reasons behind the fervent faith placed in her predictions as well as the arguments against her credibility. This dichotomy between belief and skepticism reflects the larger human tendency to seek meaning in the unknown while simultaneously questioning the sources of those meanings.

The Believers: Devotion to a Mystic's Vision

Baba Vanga's followers believe fervently in her prophetic abilities, pointing to the accuracy of many of her predictions as evidence of her gift. These believers are drawn to her mystical powers and see her as a bridge between the spiritual realm and the physical world. For them, Baba Vanga's blindness is symbolic—her inability to see the material world only enhanced her ability to see beyond it, into the future and into deeper truths about human existence.

For her followers, key reasons for their belief include:

Perceived Accuracy of Predictions: Many of Baba Vanga's devotees cite specific prophecies they believe have come true. Among the most commonly referenced are her predictions about the September 11 attacks, where she allegedly foresaw "two steel birds" hitting America, and her prediction about the 2004 Indian Ocean tsunami, where she warned of a "great wave" bringing destruction. Followers argue that these predictions are too specific to be dismissed as mere coincidence.

Spiritual Connection: Baba Vanga's followers view her as more than just a prophet; she is seen as a spiritual figure who could provide guidance, healing, and solace. People who visited her during her lifetime often reported that she seemed to know intimate details about their lives without being told. This personalized insight strengthened their belief in her abilities and fostered a deep emotional connection to her.

Mystical Aura: Baba Vanga's blindness, combined with her rural, humble origins, contributed to the mystical aura surrounding her. Many of her followers believe that her blindness allowed her to "see" beyond the material world and into realms that others could not access. This mysticism only adds to her followers' belief in her as a spiritual guide and prophet, reinforcing the idea that she had special access to knowledge hidden from ordinary people.

Cultural and Regional Reverence: Baba Vanga holds a particularly revered status in her home country of Bulgaria and in the broader Balkans region. Her status as a folk figure, as well as her association with local traditions of mysticism and prophecy, has earned her a devoted following. In these regions, her legacy continues to be honored, with many people making pilgrimages to the places she lived and worked.

The Sceptics: Doubts and Criticism

On the opposite end of the spectrum are the sceptics, who view Baba Vanga's prophecies with suspicion and often attribute her "successes" to a combination of vague language, selective memory, and coincidence. Critics argue that many of her predictions are either too general to be considered prophetic or are attributed to her only after the events have occurred. The skepticism around Baba Vanga's prophecies is grounded in a broader tradition of critical thinking and rational inquiry into the claims of mystics and prophets.

Key arguments from Baba Vanga's critics include:

Vagueness of Predictions: One of the primary criticisms leveled against Baba Vanga is that many of her predictions are too vague or symbolic to be considered reliable forecasts. For example, her description of "two steel birds" crashing into buildings in America could be applied to many different events, not just the 9/11 attacks. Critics argue that her predictions often lack specific details, which makes it easy for believers to retroactively apply them to various events.

Retrofitting Prophecies: Sceptics point out that many of Baba Vanga's so-called accurate predictions were only linked to specific events after they occurred. This practice of retrofitting prophecies—interpreting vague or cryptic statements to match events in hindsight—is a common critique of many mystical prophecies. In the case of Baba Vanga, sceptics argue that her followers often reinterpret her statements to fit major world events, making it impossible to verify whether she truly foresaw them.

No Verifiable Record of Predictions: Another point of contention is the lack of verifiable records for many of Baba Vanga's most famous predictions. Much of what is attributed to her comes from oral accounts, second-hand sources, or stories passed down by her followers, rather than documented evidence. This makes it difficult to assess the accuracy of her predictions and raises questions about how much of what is attributed to her was actually said before the events took place.

Cultural Context and Influence: Some critics argue that Baba Vanga's rise to prominence was influenced by the social and cultural context in which she lived. During the Soviet era, there was significant interest in mysticism and paranormal phenomena, which may have contributed to the spread of stories about her abilities. Sceptics suggest that her prophecies should be viewed in the context of the political and social environment of the time, rather than as evidence of supernatural foresight.

THE INTERSECTION OF Belief and Skepticism

The divide between believers and sceptics when it comes to Baba Vanga highlights a broader tension between mysticism and rationality. On one hand, many people are drawn to figures like Baba Vanga because they offer a sense of order, purpose, and guidance in an often chaotic and unpredictable world. Prophets and mystics provide hope, comfort, and a belief in forces beyond human comprehension. On the other hand, sceptics argue that relying on such figures can lead to confirmation bias, misinformation, and misplaced trust in unfounded claims.

This tension between belief and skepticism reflects deeper questions about the nature of prophecy, human psychology, and our desire for certainty in uncertain times. For many, the allure of mysticism lies in the sense of connection it provides to a higher power or greater cosmic plan. Sceptics, meanwhile, emphasize the importance of evidence, critical thinking, and the need to guard against the influence of vague or unsubstantiated claims.

The Role of Prophets in Modern Society

The debate over Baba Vanga's prophecies speaks to the broader role of prophets and seers in modern society. Throughout history, people have looked to individuals who claim to have access to divine or mystical knowledge, whether through visions, dreams, or other forms of spiritual insight. Figures like Nostradamus, Edgar Cayce, and Baba Vanga have attracted widespread followings because they offer a narrative that promises to explain the future or provide guidance in troubled times.

In an age where science and technology dominate much of public discourse, the continued influence of mystics like Baba Vanga may seem surprising. However, their appeal lies in the fact that they speak to a universal human desire for answers, particularly during times of crisis or uncertainty. As political, environmental, and social challenges continue to mount, figures like Baba Vanga offer a sense of comfort by suggesting that the future can be known, even if it cannot always be changed.

The Legacy of Baba Vanga

Whether viewed as a true prophet or simply a product of cultural and historical forces, Baba Vanga's legacy endures. Her predictions continue to capture the imagination of people around the world, and debates about her abilities persist among both her followers and her detractors. For believers, she represents a unique and powerful spiritual figure whose insights offer a glimpse into the mysteries of the universe. For sceptics, she is a reminder of the need for critical thinking and caution when it comes to unverified claims.

Ultimately, the legacy of Baba Vanga reflects the enduring human fascination with prophecy and the search for meaning in a complex and unpredictable world. Her followers find comfort and guidance in her visions, while her critics challenge the veracity of her predictions and the mechanisms by which they are interpreted.

Conclusion: The Balance between Faith and Reason

The divide between Baba Vanga's followers and sceptics illustrates the larger balance between faith and reason, mysticism and rationality. As we navigate a world filled with uncertainty and challenges, figures like Baba Vanga offer two contrasting paths: belief in forces beyond our understanding or reliance on critical thinking and empirical evidence. Each side of the debate reflects a different aspect of human nature—the need for spiritual connection and the quest for knowledge.

In this chapter, we explored the passionate devotion of Baba Vanga's believers and the reasoned skepticism of her critics. Whether viewed as a mystic or a product of cultural myth, Baba Vanga's place in modern society reflects the timeless struggle to make sense of the future and the unknown. Her legacy endures as a symbol of both the power of belief and the importance of questioning the world around us.

The Soviet Connection: How Leaders Sought Baba Vanga's Counsel

Baba Vanga's rise to fame as a prophet and mystic was not confined to her local community or even Bulgaria. Her reputation spread far beyond her homeland, capturing the attention of political figures, including some of the most powerful leaders of the Soviet Union and Eastern Europe. In a region where mysticism, folklore, and spirituality maintained a strong influence, even in the face of state-imposed atheism, Baba Vanga's prophetic abilities drew the interest of high-ranking officials, who sought her counsel on matters of political and personal significance.

In this chapter, we explore Baba Vanga's connection to Soviet and Eastern European leaders, examining how her prophecies were interpreted and utilized within the context of Cold War politics. This exploration reveals a fascinating intersection between mysticism and political power, and how even the most skeptical of regimes sometimes turned to spiritual figures for guidance in times of uncertainty.

Baba Vanga's Reputation in the Soviet Bloc

Baba Vanga's reputation as a mystic with the ability to foresee the future and provide insight into personal and political matters began to grow during the mid-20th century. As word of her prophecies spread across Bulgaria, she quickly attracted a diverse group of followers that included ordinary people seeking personal advice and powerful figures from the Soviet and Eastern European elite.

Despite the Soviet Union's official stance on atheism and its promotion of scientific materialism, there was a surprising tolerance for mysticism and paranormal phenomena among some sectors of the political establishment. The KGB, for instance, is known to have explored paranormal research, including experiments with telepathy and psychic abilities, as part of their broader efforts to understand and harness unconventional sources of power.

In this climate, Baba Vanga's growing reputation as a mystic made her a figure of interest to Soviet and Eastern European leaders. Her prophecies, which often touched on political events, world leaders, and the future of communism, offered a potential source of insight for those navigating the complex and often precarious world of Cold War politics.

The Role of Mysticism in Soviet-Era Politics

The interest in Baba Vanga's prophecies reflects a broader phenomenon in Soviet and Eastern European politics, where mysticism, despite being officially discouraged, remained influential behind closed doors. Leaders in the Soviet Union and its satellite states often found themselves grappling with the uncertainties of political power, international conflict, and economic instability, and it was not uncommon for them to seek guidance from unconventional sources.

THE SOVIET INTEREST in the Paranormal: During the height of the Cold War, the Soviet government secretly funded research into paranormal abilities, including psychic phenomena, telekinesis, and remote viewing. This research was driven by a desire to gain an advantage over the West in intelligence gathering and psychological warfare. Although much of this work remained hidden from public view, it demonstrated that even the staunchly secular Soviet state was not immune to the allure of mysticism and the unknown.

Political Uncertainty and Prophecy: For leaders in the Soviet bloc, the future was often fraught with uncertainty. Political purges, international crises, and economic challenges were constant threats to stability. In this context, figures like Baba Vanga, who claimed to have access to knowledge of the future, were seen as potential sources of guidance. Although these leaders may not have publicly acknowledged their reliance on mystics, many are believed to have sought Baba Vanga's counsel in private.

Baba Vanga and the Communist Leadership

Baba Vanga's connection to the Soviet and Eastern European leadership extended beyond her general reputation as a prophet. There are several reports of high-ranking officials, including leaders from Bulgaria and the Soviet Union, seeking her advice on both personal and political matters.

Todor Zhivkov, Bulgarian Leader: One of the most notable examples of a political figure seeking Baba Vanga's counsel was Todor Zhivkov, the longtime leader of Communist Bulgaria. Zhivkov reportedly visited Baba Vanga on multiple occasions, asking for her insight into political decisions and the future of Bulgaria. According to some accounts, he valued her advice and saw her as a trusted advisor, despite the Communist Party's official stance on religion and mysticism.

Soviet Leaders and Baba Vanga: There are also rumors that several Soviet leaders, including members of the KGB, consulted with Baba Vanga during times of political crisis. Although these consultations were likely kept secret to avoid contradicting the Soviet Union's official ideology, it is believed that her reputation for foresight made her an attractive figure for those seeking answers to complex political problems.

The Personal and the Political: Baba Vanga's influence was not limited to grand political matters. Many of the leaders who visited her also sought advice on personal issues, such as family matters, health, and relationships. This dual role—offering both political guidance and personal insight—strengthened her bond with the political elite and solidified her status as a trusted and respected figure.

Prophecies and Political Predictions

One of the reasons Baba Vanga attracted the attention of Soviet and Eastern European leaders was her reputation for accurately predicting political events. Over the course of her life, she made several prophecies that were interpreted as predictions of key political developments in the Soviet bloc and beyond.

The Fall of the Soviet Union: Perhaps one of Baba Vanga's most famous political prophecies was her prediction of the collapse of the Soviet Union. She reportedly foresaw that the communist regime in Russia would come to an end, leading to the dissolution of the USSR and the rise of a new political order. For many of her followers, this prediction, which appeared to come true with the fall of the Berlin Wall in 1989 and the breakup of the Soviet Union in 1991, reinforced her status as a legitimate prophet.

The Reunification of Germany: Another of Baba Vanga's political predictions involved the reunification of East and West Germany. She is said to have foreseen the collapse of the Berlin Wall and the eventual reunification of the country, which took place in 1990. This prophecy, like her prediction of the Soviet Union's collapse, resonated deeply with those living in Eastern Europe and further cemented her reputation as a seer who could foresee the future of geopolitics.

Conflicts and Revolutions: Baba Vanga also made several predictions about conflicts and revolutions in Eastern Europe, some of which were seen as warnings to the Soviet leadership. She foresaw uprisings and political unrest in countries like Romania, where Nicolae Ceaușescu's brutal dictatorship was overthrown in a violent revolution in 1989. For many, these prophecies were further evidence of her ability to predict major political changes in the region.

Skepticism and Secrecy

Despite her popularity with some leaders, Baba Vanga's connection to the Soviet and Eastern European leadership was not without its critics. Within the official circles of the Communist Party, many remained deeply skeptical of her abilities and viewed her influence as a threat to the state's secular ideology. The Communist Party promoted scientific materialism and rejected religious or mystical beliefs, and Baba Vanga's growing popularity ran counter to these values.

For this reason, many of Baba Vanga's interactions with political leaders were kept secret, with only limited information about these meetings being made public. While some leaders may have sought her counsel in private, they were careful to avoid any public acknowledgment of her influence, fearing the potential backlash from party officials and the public.

Baba Vanga's Enduring Influence

Even after the fall of the Soviet Union and the end of the Cold War, Baba Vanga's influence on political figures and leaders in Eastern Europe has endured. Her prophecies continue to captivate the public, and many political figures still invoke her predictions in discussions about the future of the region. While the Soviet Union may no longer exist, the mystique surrounding Baba Vanga's role in its history remains a source of fascination for many.

In the years since her death, her legacy has been preserved through books, documentaries, and continued interest in her life and predictions. Her prophecies about the future—ranging from the environmental collapse to humanity's encounters with extraterrestrial life—continue to inspire debate and discussion.

Conclusion: Mysticism and Power in the Soviet Era

Baba Vanga's relationship with Soviet and Eastern European leaders reveals a surprising intersection between mysticism and political power during the Cold War. Despite the official atheist stance of the Communist Party, leaders and officials found themselves drawn to Baba Vanga's prophetic abilities, seeking her counsel on matters both personal and political. Her reputation as a trusted advisor to figures like Todor Zhivkov and others highlights the enduring influence of mysticism in a region that, at least officially, rejected the supernatural.

In this chapter, we explored how Baba Vanga's prophecies became intertwined with the political landscape of the Soviet Union and its satellite states. Her predictions about the fall of the Soviet Union, the reunification of Germany, and political uprisings in Eastern Europe made her a figure of immense importance to those navigating the turbulent world of Cold War politics. While some sought her guidance in secret, her influence on the region's leaders is a testament to the power of prophecy—even in the most skeptical of regimes.

Baba Vanga and the Paranormal: Beyond the Physical Realm

Baba Vanga's reputation as a mystic and prophet is deeply intertwined with the paranormal. Her unique abilities were said to extend far beyond simple predictions of future events; she reportedly had access to spiritual and metaphysical realms, communicating with unseen forces and gaining insights into events and phenomena that lay outside the bounds of the physical world. Her followers claim that Baba Vanga's connection to the paranormal allowed her to tap into hidden knowledge, foresee world-changing events, and provide guidance on matters both personal and global.

In this chapter, we explore Baba Vanga's relationship with the paranormal, examining the various dimensions of her abilities that went beyond the material world. From claims of psychic visions and spiritual communication to her knowledge of mysterious entities, we delve into the stories that have made Baba Vanga a figure of both awe and mystery. We also consider how her connection to the paranormal has contributed to her enduring legacy as a mystic and spiritual guide.

Psychic Visions: Seeing Beyond the Physical

One of the most well-known aspects of Baba Vanga's abilities was her psychic vision. Despite being physically blind from a young age, Baba Vanga was believed to possess the ability to see beyond the physical world. Her "sight" was not tied to the material realm but was instead connected to spiritual and metaphysical dimensions. She often described her visions as scenes unfolding in her mind's eye, offering glimpses of events yet to happen or providing insights into the spiritual conditions of people who visited her.

Baba Vanga's followers claim that her psychic visions allowed her to:

Foresee Global Events: Many of her predictions about world events, such as the September 11 attacks, the 2004 tsunami, and the collapse of the Soviet Union, are said to have come to her through psychic visions. These visions were often symbolic in nature, with Baba Vanga interpreting the metaphors and images she saw to offer warnings about future events.

Diagnose Illnesses: Baba Vanga was also believed to have the ability to diagnose physical ailments through her psychic sight. Visitors would come to her with health concerns, and without touching or examining them, she would provide diagnoses that many claimed were accurate. Her spiritual insight into the human body was said to be one of her most impressive abilities, leading many people to seek her help when conventional medicine failed.

Connect to the Past and Future: Baba Vanga's psychic visions were not limited to the present moment. She reportedly had access to both the past and the future, allowing her to provide detailed insights into historical events as well as foresee long-term future occurrences. Her visions spanned centuries, which is why many of her prophecies extend far into the future, with some focusing on events set to occur in the 22nd, 30th, and even 51st centuries.

Spiritual Communication: Connecting with Other Realms

Beyond her psychic abilities, Baba Vanga was believed to communicate with spiritual entities and forces that existed beyond the physical plane. She often spoke of her connection to unseen beings, spirits, and energies, describing how they provided her with knowledge and insight into events that could not be perceived through ordinary means.

Baba Vanga's communication with the spiritual realm included:

Guides and Protectors: Baba Vanga claimed that she was in contact with spiritual guides who helped her interpret the visions she received. These guides, according to her, were benevolent beings who assisted her in accessing knowledge from other dimensions and realms. She often referred to these entities as her protectors, ensuring that the information she provided was accurate and helpful to those who sought her counsel.

Communicating with the Deceased: Many of Baba Vanga's visitors believed that she had the ability to communicate with deceased loved ones. According to reports, she could relay messages from the dead, providing comfort to grieving families and helping them find closure. Her ability to bridge the gap between the living and the dead further reinforced her mystical reputation and attracted people from all walks of life.

Warnings from the Spiritual Realm: Baba Vanga frequently mentioned receiving warnings from the spiritual realm about future dangers and disasters. These warnings often came in the form of visions or messages from otherworldly entities, urging her to alert humanity to the risks of war, environmental destruction, and moral decline. Her prophecies were sometimes presented as direct communications from these spiritual forces, with Baba Vanga acting as a messenger for a higher power.

Encounters with the Paranormal: The Unseen World

In addition to her psychic visions and spiritual communication, Baba Vanga reportedly had numerous encounters with the paranormal—experiences that defied explanation and reinforced her connection to the unseen world. These encounters, shared by her followers and those who visited her, provide a glimpse into the more mysterious aspects of her life.

Premonitions and Omens: Baba Vanga often experienced premonitions and omens, which she interpreted as signs of impending events. These signs were not always visual; they sometimes manifested as physical sensations, sounds, or changes in the atmosphere around her. For example, she claimed that before a significant event or tragedy, she would feel a shift in energy or hear strange noises, which signaled that something important was about to occur.

Poltergeist Activity: Some of Baba Vanga's visitors reported witnessing strange occurrences when they were in her presence, such as objects moving on their own, unexplained noises, or lights flickering. While these phenomena were rare, they contributed to the belief that Baba Vanga had a connection to the paranormal and could influence the physical world through her spiritual powers.

Prophetic Dreams: In addition to her waking visions, Baba Vanga frequently received messages through dreams. These dreams were often vivid and symbolic, offering her detailed information about events that were yet to happen. For her, dreams were another means of accessing hidden knowledge, and she often encouraged her followers to pay attention to their own dreams as a source of guidance.

Mystical Entities and Forces

Baba Vanga's connection to the paranormal extended beyond human spirits and spiritual guides. She often spoke of encounters with mystical entities and forces that were neither human nor divine but existed in the hidden realms of the universe. According to her, these entities were part of a larger cosmic order that shaped the fate of humanity and the world.

Extraterrestrial Beings: One of Baba Vanga's most intriguing paranormal claims was her belief in extraterrestrial life. She predicted that humanity would make contact with aliens in the 22nd century and described these beings as intelligent, advanced civilizations that had been watching Earth for centuries. While her descriptions of these entities were often vague, she believed that they played a role in the evolution of humanity and would eventually reveal themselves.

Elemental Forces: Baba Vanga also believed in the existence of elemental forces that governed natural phenomena. These forces, according to her, could be harnessed or disrupted by human actions, and their influence was felt in environmental disasters, such as earthquakes, storms, and droughts. She often warned that humanity's disregard for nature would provoke these elemental forces, leading to devastating consequences.

Interdimensional Entities: In addition to extraterrestrial beings and elemental forces, Baba Vanga claimed to have knowledge of interdimensional entities that existed outside the normal boundaries of space and time. These entities, she suggested, had the ability to move between dimensions and influence the events of the physical world. While she did not often speak of these beings in detail, her references to them added to the sense of mystery surrounding her paranormal abilities.

Skeptical Views on Baba Vanga's Paranormal Abilities

As with her prophecies, Baba Vanga's paranormal abilities have been met with both belief and skepticism. Critics argue that many of the stories surrounding her encounters with the spiritual and paranormal realm are exaggerated or fabricated by her followers, while others suggest that her abilities can be explained through psychological phenomena rather than supernatural forces.

Psychological Explanation: Some sceptics suggest that Baba Vanga's experiences with the paranormal could be explained by psychological factors, such as heightened intuition, pattern recognition, and suggestibility. They argue that her ability to provide accurate diagnoses or foresee events may have been the result of her keen observational skills, rather than paranormal abilities.

THE POWER OF BELIEF: Sceptics also point to the power of belief in shaping people's perceptions of Baba Vanga's abilities. Many of her visitors came to her with a strong belief in her powers, and this belief may have influenced their interpretation of their experiences with her. In this view, the paranormal phenomena associated with Baba Vanga are less about her actual abilities and more about the expectations and desires of her followers.

Conclusion: Baba Vanga's Paranormal Legacy

Baba Vanga's connection to the paranormal has played a central role in her enduring legacy as a mystic and spiritual guide. Her abilities to see beyond the physical world, communicate with spiritual entities, and encounter unseen forces have made her a figure of fascination and reverence for believers around the world. Whether viewed as a gifted prophet or a product of cultural myth, Baba Vanga's relationship with the paranormal continues to captivate those who seek to understand the mysteries of the universe.

In this chapter, we explored the various dimensions of Baba Vanga's paranormal abilities, from her psychic visions to her encounters with otherworldly entities. Her experiences offer a glimpse into a world beyond the material, where forces unseen by most shape the course of human events. While her abilities remain a subject of debate, there is no doubt that

Baba Vanga's connection to the paranormal has contributed to her lasting influence and the mystical aura that surrounds her legacy.

Visions of the Future: How Baba Vanga's Prophecies Outlive Her

Baba Vanga's prophecies have a unique and enduring quality that continues to captivate people long after her death in 1996. Her visions, which spanned centuries and extended far beyond her lifetime, remain a source of fascination for both her followers and curious onlookers alike. These predictions cover a wide range of topics, from political upheavals and natural disasters to technological advancements and humanity's future encounters with extraterrestrial beings. For many, Baba Vanga's prophetic legacy is seen not only in the events that have already come to pass but also in the future scenarios she envisioned that have yet to unfold.

In this chapter, we explore the ways in which Baba Vanga's prophecies continue to outlive her, shaping contemporary discussions about the future. We will examine the major themes of her visions, why they continue to resonate in today's world, and how they are interpreted and reinterpreted as new events emerge. Her ability to project beyond her own time and offer glimpses of distant future events has ensured that her legacy as a prophet remains as powerful as ever.

A Visionary for the Ages: Prophecies That Transcend Time

Baba Vanga's prophecies are remarkable for their scope, spanning centuries into the future and touching on almost every aspect of human life. Unlike many mystics whose predictions are confined to their own lifetimes, Baba Vanga's visions extend well beyond her death, with many events she foretold expected to unfold centuries from now.

Her prophecies include predictions of:

Technological Advancements: Baba Vanga foresaw rapid advancements in technology that would change the way humans live and interact with the world. Some of her predictions involve artificial intelligence, space travel, and the development of new energy sources. One of her more dramatic predictions includes the use of technology to explore Venus by 2028, a claim that aligns with humanity's growing interest in space exploration.

Global Environmental Crisis: Baba Vanga's environmental prophecies are some of the most striking. She predicted that rising sea levels, extreme weather events, and natural disasters would increase as humanity failed to respect the Earth's natural balance. Her vision of a world struggling with the consequences of climate change resonates powerfully today as governments, scientists, and activists grapple with global warming and environmental degradation.

Political Revolutions and Global Shifts: Baba Vanga also foresaw significant political changes, including revolutions, the rise and fall of empires, and new geopolitical orders. For instance, she predicted the return of communism on a global scale by 2076 and the collapse of the European population due to conflict in 2025, events that continue to be subjects of debate and speculation among her followers.

Extraterrestrial Contact: One of Baba Vanga's more ambitious predictions is that humanity will make contact with extraterrestrial beings by 2130, ushering in a new era of cosmic understanding. She envisioned these encounters as transformative for humanity, leading to shifts in how we understand ourselves and our place in the universe.

Baba Vanga's ability to foresee events far into the future has allowed her legacy to endure. Her prophecies serve as touchstones for those seeking to understand or prepare for the future, particularly in an era marked by uncertainty and rapid change.

Themes That Resonate in the Modern World

Baba Vanga's prophecies touch on themes that remain highly relevant to contemporary society. Her visions of environmental collapse, political instability, and technological advancement all mirror the challenges and opportunities that humanity faces today. This resonance with modern concerns ensures that her prophecies continue to be discussed and analyzed, even decades after her death.

Environmental Warnings: Baba Vanga's warnings about the environment are perhaps the most poignant for today's world. As climate change accelerates and the impacts of environmental degradation become more visible, her prophecies about melting ice caps, widespread droughts, and natural disasters seem eerily prescient. Her prediction of catastrophic environmental events aligns with current scientific projections, making her a figure of interest for those concerned with climate issues.

Technological Transformation: The rapid pace of technological innovation has made Baba Vanga's predictions about future advancements particularly relevant. As artificial intelligence, robotics, and space exploration continue to evolve, her vision of a highly technologically advanced future no longer seems far-fetched. For many, her prophecies offer insight into the possibilities and ethical dilemmas that technology may bring.

Political Upheaval: Baba Vanga's prophecies of political revolutions and shifts in global power have also gained renewed interest in light of recent political instability. The rise of populist movements, growing tensions between global powers, and concerns about economic inequality all echo the political changes she foresaw. Her vision of a new world order—marked by significant political realignments—speaks to ongoing anxieties about the future of governance and democracy.

These enduring themes ensure that Baba Vanga's prophecies remain a focal point for those seeking to make sense of the present and anticipate the future.

How Prophecies Are Reinterpreted Over Time

One of the reasons Baba Vanga's prophecies have such staying power is the way they are reinterpreted and adapted as new events unfold. While some of her predictions are viewed as direct and specific (such as her alleged forewarning of the 9/11 attacks), others are more open to interpretation. As a result, her followers often revisit her prophecies in the wake of significant global events, seeking to find new meanings or connections.

For example:

Environmental Crises: As climate change has become more widely acknowledged, many have reexamined Baba Vanga's prophecies about rising sea levels, extreme weather, and environmental degradation. Her warnings have taken on new urgency in light of recent disasters, such as wildfires, hurricanes, and droughts. Some followers believe that her visions may offer clues about future environmental tipping points.

Political Predictions: Baba Vanga's predictions about political upheaval, including the collapse of European populations and the rise of new global powers, are constantly being revisited in the context of contemporary events. Political crises, such as Brexit or tensions in Eastern Europe, are sometimes linked to her prophecies, with followers debating whether these events are the beginnings of the changes she foresaw.

Technological Development: With the rise of AI, space exploration, and new energy technologies, Baba Vanga's predictions about future scientific breakthroughs are also being reinterpreted. For instance, her prediction of human exploration of Venus is seen as aligning with renewed interest in space travel, particularly missions to Mars and beyond.

This process of reinterpretation ensures that Baba Vanga's prophecies remain relevant as new events arise. Her followers view her predictions as living documents, evolving with the times and offering continuous insight into the challenges and opportunities of the future.

The Role of Faith in Baba Vanga's Legacy

Belief in Baba Vanga's prophecies is deeply intertwined with the role of faith. For her followers, she is not just a prophet but a spiritual guide whose visions provide a framework for understanding the world. Even when her prophecies seem distant or uncertain, her believers maintain a strong sense of trust in her abilities, viewing her predictions as divinely inspired or connected to higher spiritual forces.

A Spiritual Framework: For many, Baba Vanga's prophecies offer more than just predictions; they provide a spiritual framework for navigating the uncertainties of life. Her warnings about moral decline, environmental collapse, and technological advancement are often seen as calls to action, urging humanity to make changes before it is too late.

Enduring Faith: The fact that many of her prophecies have yet to come to pass does not diminish the faith of her followers. Instead, they see her predictions as unfolding in their own time, with the understanding that some events may not occur for centuries. This enduring faith in her abilities ensures that her prophecies continue to influence those who seek her guidance.

Skepticism and Debate around Baba Vanga's Visions

While Baba Vanga's prophecies have inspired devotion, they have also been the subject of significant skepticism. Critics argue that many of her predictions are either too vague to be meaningful or retroactively applied to events. In particular, sceptics point to the lack of verifiable records for some of her most famous predictions and the tendency for her followers to reinterpret her prophecies in light of contemporary events.

Retrofitting Events: Sceptics often accuse Baba Vanga's followers of retrofitting her predictions to match events after they occur. For example, while many claim that she predicted the 9/11 attacks, the specifics of her prophecy are often vague and open to interpretation. Critics argue that such prophecies can be applied to a wide range of events, making them less impressive as predictions.

Ambiguity and Symbolism: Another point of contention is the ambiguity and symbolic nature of many of Baba Vanga's prophecies. Her use of metaphorical language, such as the "two steel birds" flying into buildings (interpreted as the 9/11 attacks), leaves much room for interpretation. This lack of specificity has led some to question the validity of her visions.

Despite the skepticism, Baba Vanga's prophecies continue to be discussed, debated, and reexamined as time progresses. Her predictions provoke both belief and doubt, ensuring that her legacy remains vibrant and controversial.

Conclusion: A Legacy That Endures

Baba Vanga's prophecies have outlived her by decades and will likely continue to be a source of fascination for centuries to come. Her ability to see far into the future, combined with the depth and breadth of her visions, ensures that her influence endures in the public imagination. Whether viewed as a gifted prophet or a figure of controversy, her legacy transcends time and continues to provoke curiosity, belief, and debate.

In this chapter, we explored how Baba Vanga's prophecies have outlived her, continuing to shape discussions about the future in an ever-changing world. Her visions of technological breakthroughs, political shifts, environmental disasters, and encounters with extraterrestrial life remain relevant to modern concerns and challenges. As her prophecies continue to be reinterpreted and reexamined, Baba Vanga's impact on the world of mysticism and prophecy remains as strong as ever.

A Century of Change: Baba Vanga's Warnings for the Next 100 Years

Baba Vanga's prophetic vision extended far beyond the events of her own lifetime, encompassing the future of humanity over the next hundred years and beyond. She issued numerous warnings about the challenges and transformations that lie ahead for the world. Her predictions touch on a wide range of themes, from technological advances and environmental disasters to political revolutions and cosmic encounters, shaping a future that, according to her, will be marked by both immense progress and grave risks.

In this chapter, we explore Baba Vanga's warnings for the next century, examining the key events and changes she foresaw. We will delve into her vision of humanity's future, focusing on the opportunities for advancement, the potential dangers, and the moral lessons her predictions offer. As we face an uncertain century, Baba Vanga's prophecies remain a topic of intrigue and a source of reflection on what the future may hold.

Technological Advancements: A Double-Edged Sword

One of the most prominent themes in Baba Vanga's predictions for the next 100 years is the rapid advancement of technology. She foresaw incredible technological breakthroughs that would revolutionize the way humans live, work, and interact with the world. However, she also issued warnings about the potential dangers of unchecked technological progress, suggesting that humanity must tread carefully to avoid catastrophic consequences.

Artificial Intelligence and Automation: Baba Vanga predicted that artificial intelligence (AI) and automation would play an increasingly dominant role in human society, transforming industries and creating new forms of labor. She envisioned a world where machines would handle many of the tasks once performed by humans, leading to higher productivity and efficiency. However, she also warned that this technological shift could lead to widespread unemployment, social unrest, and a loss of human connection if not managed responsibly.

Medical Advances and Longevity: According to Baba Vanga, the next century will see remarkable advances in medicine, with new treatments and cures for previously untreatable diseases. She predicted that medical technology would extend human life spans significantly, allowing people to live much longer and healthier lives. Despite this optimistic outlook, she cautioned that the ethical implications of such advancements—such as population growth and inequality in access to healthcare—must be carefully considered.

Space Exploration and Colonization: Baba Vanga also foresaw major breakthroughs in space exploration, including the colonization of other planets. She predicted that by the middle of the 21st century, humanity would begin exploring Venus and Mars in search of resources and new frontiers for human civilization. While this exploration offers hope for the survival of humanity in the face of environmental decline, Baba Vanga warned that space exploration would not come without challenges, including the potential for conflict with extraterrestrial civilizations.

Environmental Collapse: A Century of Crisis

Baba Vanga's warnings about the environment are among her most urgent and dire prophecies for the next century. She predicted that humanity's continued exploitation of natural resources and disregard for the environment would lead to catastrophic consequences, resulting in widespread destruction, loss of biodiversity, and extreme weather events.

Melting Ice Caps and Rising Sea Levels: One of her most notable environmental predictions involves the rapid melting of the polar ice caps, leading to drastic rises in sea levels. Baba Vanga warned that by the mid-21st century, many coastal cities and regions would be submerged, forcing mass migrations and creating humanitarian crises. This prophecy aligns with current scientific predictions about the impact of climate change, making it one of her most widely discussed warnings.

Extreme Weather and Natural Disasters: Baba Vanga foresaw an increase in extreme weather events, including hurricanes, droughts, and wildfires, as a result of climate change. She warned that these disasters would become more frequent and severe, overwhelming governments and communities unprepared for their impact. Her prophecy suggests that the next century will be marked by environmental instability, with entire ecosystems at risk of collapse.

Global Water and Food Shortages: Another key environmental warning from Baba Vanga involves the depletion of vital resources, particularly fresh water and arable land. She predicted that as the global population grows and the environment deteriorates, access to clean water and food will become increasingly scarce. This, in turn, could lead to conflict and geopolitical tensions, as nations compete for dwindling resources.

Political and Social Upheaval: A New World Order

Baba Vanga's vision for the next century also includes major political and social changes, with the potential for both progress and disruption. She predicted that the current world order would be significantly reshaped by revolutions, conflicts, and the rise of new political ideologies.

The Return of Communism: One of Baba Vanga's most surprising predictions is the return of communism on a global scale by 2076. She foresaw a new form of communism emerging, not as a violent revolution but as a result of societal shifts toward equality and shared resources. According to her vision, the failures of capitalism and increasing economic inequality would push humanity toward a system based on collective ownership and wealth redistribution. While this prophecy remains speculative, it reflects ongoing debates about the future of economic systems in an era of automation and wealth disparity.

Global Conflicts and Revolutions: Baba Vanga also warned of political instability and conflict, particularly in Europe. She predicted that a major conflict in Europe would devastate the continent's population by 2025, leading to widespread social and economic upheaval. This conflict, according to her prophecy, would act as a catalyst for broader geopolitical changes, including the rise of new powers and the decline of existing ones.

A Shift in Global Power: Baba Vanga foresaw significant changes in global leadership over the next century, with some nations rising to prominence while others face decline. She predicted that China and other Asian countries would continue to grow in power and influence, potentially leading the way in technological innovation and global governance. At the same time, she warned that traditional Western powers, particularly Europe and the United States, would face internal divisions and challenges that could undermine their global standing.

Moral and Spiritual Warnings: A Call for Human Change

Baba Vanga's predictions for the next century are not only about external events but also about the moral and spiritual choices humanity must make. She warned that without a shift in values—toward greater empathy, cooperation, and respect for nature—humanity would continue to face suffering and hardship. Her prophecies serve as a call to action, urging people to reconsider their relationship with each other and the planet.

A New Age of Enlightenment: While many of her predictions are dire, Baba Vanga also foresaw the possibility of a new age of enlightenment, where humanity evolves beyond conflict and materialism to embrace spiritual growth and unity. She believed that the hardships of the next century would ultimately push people to seek deeper meaning and connection, leading to a global awakening. This vision offers hope for a future where humans live in harmony with nature and each other.

The Dangers of Materialism: Baba Vanga frequently warned against the dangers of materialism, predicting that humanity's obsession with wealth and power would lead to moral decay. She believed that this focus on material success would contribute to the environmental and social crises of the next century and that only by turning toward spiritual values could humanity find peace and balance.

The Role of Love and Compassion: Central to Baba Vanga's moral vision for the future is the importance of love and compassion. She often spoke of the need for greater empathy and understanding in human relationships, predicting that only by fostering compassion could people overcome the divisions and conflicts that threaten to tear society apart. Her prophecy suggests that the next century will be defined by the struggle between love and fear, with the future depending on which force prevails.

Humanity's Encounter with the Unknown: Extraterrestrial Contact

One of Baba Vanga's most extraordinary predictions for the next century involves humanity's contact with extraterrestrial civilizations. According to her prophecy, by the year 2130, humans will establish communication with intelligent life from other planets, leading to profound changes in our understanding of the universe and our place in it.

The Role of Extraterrestrial Beings: Baba Vanga predicted that extraterrestrial beings would not only make contact with humanity but also play a role in guiding human progress. She believed that these beings possessed advanced technology and knowledge that could help humans address some of the major challenges facing the planet, such as environmental degradation and resource shortages.

A New Cosmic Perspective: The encounter with extraterrestrial civilizations, according to Baba Vanga, would fundamentally alter humanity's worldview, leading to a shift in how we understand life, intelligence, and the cosmos. She predicted that this encounter would usher in a new era of cooperation and exploration, as humans and extraterrestrials work together to expand knowledge and solve global problems.

Potential Conflicts: Despite the potential for positive collaboration, Baba Vanga also warned that contact with extraterrestrials could lead to conflict, particularly if humans approach these encounters with fear or aggression. She urged humanity to embrace a mindset of openness and curiosity, rather than fear, in order to avoid misunderstandings and conflict with other intelligent beings.

Conclusion: The Next 100 Years as Foreseen by Baba Vanga

Baba Vanga's warnings for the next century paint a picture of a world on the brink of transformation. Her prophecies encompass both incredible advancements and dire challenges, offering a vision of a future where humanity must confront the consequences of its actions and make critical choices about its path forward. Whether predicting technological breakthroughs, environmental disasters, political upheaval, or cosmic encounters, her vision for the next 100 years serves as both a warning and a source of hope.

In this chapter, we explored Baba Vanga's predictions for the next century, examining the key events and themes she foresaw. As we move deeper into the 21st century, her prophecies continue to resonate, offering a unique lens through which to view the challenges and opportunities that lie ahead. Whether one believes in her prophetic abilities or not, Baba Vanga's vision of the future offers valuable insights into the moral, social, and environmental choices humanity must confront as we navigate the coming decades.

Humanity's Survival: The Long, Drawn-Out Apocalypse

One of Baba Vanga's most intriguing and unsettling prophecies involves what she described as a "drawn-out apocalypse," a series of events that would gradually lead to the collapse of civilization as we know it. Unlike the instant, catastrophic end-of-the-world scenarios found in many doomsday predictions, Baba Vanga foresaw a slow, agonizing decline in the 21st century and beyond—one marked by environmental disasters, social upheaval, political instability, and humanity's struggle to adapt and survive. Despite these challenges, she also hinted that this prolonged apocalypse would not mean the total extinction of humanity, but rather a period of transformation, survival, and perhaps eventual renewal.

In this chapter, we examine Baba Vanga's concept of the long, drawn-out apocalypse. We will explore the key stages she predicted for this gradual collapse and the factors that will contribute to humanity's struggle. Finally, we consider what her prophecy suggests about humanity's resilience and the potential for recovery, even in the face of overwhelming odds.

The Beginning of the End: Conflict and Division

Baba Vanga predicted that the slow apocalypse would begin with increasing conflict and division among human societies, driven by political, economic, and ideological differences. According to her, humanity's inability to reconcile its differences would lead to a series of conflicts that would destabilize entire regions, particularly in Europe, where she foresaw a devastating war as early as 2025.

Conflict in Europe: Baba Vanga predicted that a major conflict in Europe would severely impact the continent, reducing its population and leading to political and social chaos. She envisioned this conflict as part of a larger pattern of global unrest, as nations struggle to maintain power and control over diminishing resources. While the specifics of this war are unclear, the ripple effects—mass migration, economic collapse, and political fragmentation—would set the stage for further global instability.

Polarization and Ideological Clashes: Beyond military conflict, Baba Vanga also foresaw deep ideological divisions within societies. She warned that growing polarization, particularly between different political, religious, and social groups, would make cooperation increasingly difficult, leading to widespread civil unrest. This division, she believed, would erode the foundations of democratic institutions and fuel populist movements, further destabilizing governments around the world.

The Collapse of Global Institutions: As conflict and division spread, Baba Vanga predicted that many of the global institutions created to maintain peace and stability—such as the United Nations and other international organizations—would weaken or collapse entirely. Without these mechanisms for cooperation and diplomacy, she warned, humanity would be left vulnerable to escalating conflicts and the breakdown of international order.

ENVIRONMENTAL DECLINE: Nature Strikes Back

Central to Baba Vanga's vision of the long apocalypse is the gradual degradation of the natural world. She predicted that the environmental damage caused by human activity—deforestation, pollution, overfishing, and climate change—would lead to a series of cascading disasters, each worsening the next, as the planet's ecosystems collapse.

Climate Change and Rising Sea Levels: Baba Vanga's most famous environmental prophecy involves the melting of the polar ice caps and the dramatic rise in sea levels. She warned that coastal cities and low-lying areas around the world would be submerged, displacing millions of people and creating massive humanitarian crises. This flooding, coupled with increasingly severe weather events like hurricanes, droughts, and wildfires, would make many parts of the world uninhabitable, forcing people to migrate in search of safer ground.

Biodiversity Loss and Ecosystem Collapse: Baba Vanga also predicted that the loss of biodiversity would accelerate as species go extinct at an unprecedented rate. With ecosystems destabilized, food chains would collapse, leading to widespread crop failures and food shortages. The resulting hunger and desperation would spark further conflicts, as nations compete for access to dwindling resources like fresh water and arable land.

Resource Depletion and Energy Crises: In her vision, humanity's reliance on finite resources—particularly fossil fuels—would lead to a global energy crisis. As energy supplies dwindle, economies would falter, and people would be forced to turn to alternative, often dangerous or untested, sources of energy. Baba Vanga warned that efforts to find new energy sources, such as exploring Venus in 2028, would come too late to prevent the worst of the environmental and economic fallout.

Technological Dependence and the Rise of AI

While Baba Vanga acknowledged that technological advancements could offer solutions to some of humanity's problems, she also issued warnings about the dangers of becoming overly reliant on technology, particularly artificial intelligence (AI). She foresaw that the rapid development of AI and automation would dramatically alter human society, leading to both progress and peril.

Automation and Unemployment: One of Baba Vanga's most pressing concerns was that the rise of automation would lead to mass unemployment, as machines replace human labor in industries ranging from manufacturing to service. She warned that without careful planning and regulation, this shift would exacerbate existing economic inequalities, leaving millions without work or access to the benefits of technological progress. The resulting social unrest could further destabilize already fragile societies.

AI and the Loss of Human Autonomy: Baba Vanga also foresaw the potential for AI to overreach its original purposes, warning that as machines grow more intelligent, they could begin to challenge human authority and autonomy. While she did not predict a scenario as dramatic as a robot uprising, she believed that humanity's increasing reliance on AI would come with significant risks—particularly if ethical considerations were ignored in the rush to develop smarter, more capable machines.

Technological Solutions to Environmental and Social Problems: Despite these warnings, Baba Vanga also saw technology as a possible means of survival during the long apocalypse. She predicted that advancements in renewable energy, space exploration, and AI-driven healthcare could help mitigate some of the worst effects of environmental collapse and social unrest. However, she emphasized that these technological solutions would only succeed if they were applied with wisdom, cooperation, and respect for the planet's natural limits.

Moral and Spiritual Decline: Humanity's Inner Apocalypse

For Baba Vanga, the drawn-out apocalypse was not just about external events; it also involved a moral and spiritual crisis within humanity itself. She believed that as societies became more materialistic, people would lose touch with the values of compassion, empathy, and cooperation, leading to a breakdown of trust and social cohesion.

The Rise of Materialism and Greed: Baba Vanga warned that humanity's obsession with wealth, power, and technological progress would come at the cost of human relationships and spiritual fulfillment. She predicted that as people became more focused on material success, they would lose sight of the importance of community and cooperation, leading to increased isolation, distrust, and conflict.

Moral Decay and Social Fragmentation: In her vision of the future, Baba Vanga foresaw a world in which moral values would be eroded, particularly in the face of environmental and economic crises. As governments and institutions fail to address these challenges, people would turn inward, prioritizing their own survival over the well-being of others. This moral decay, she warned, would exacerbate the social fragmentation already caused by political and ideological divisions, making it even harder for humanity to come together to address the larger existential threats it faces.

The Loss of Spiritual Connection: Baba Vanga believed that humanity's spiritual disconnection from nature and from each other would be a key factor in the drawn-out apocalypse. She warned that people would become increasingly disconnected from the natural world, viewing it as a resource to be exploited rather than something to be cherished and protected. Without a spiritual awakening, she predicted, humanity would continue down a path of self-destruction.

Humanity's Struggle for Survival: Adapting to a Changed World

Despite the grim outlook, Baba Vanga's prophecy of a long apocalypse was not entirely devoid of hope. She foresaw that even as civilization crumbles, humanity would find ways to adapt and survive, though this survival would come at a great cost.

Migration and New Settlements: As sea levels rise and natural disasters make parts of the world uninhabitable, Baba Vanga predicted that large-scale migrations would reshape the global population. Entire nations would be forced to relocate, with many fleeing to higher ground or seeking refuge in parts of the world that are less affected by climate change. This mass movement of people would create new tensions but also new opportunities for cooperation and rebuilding.

Survival through Innovation: Baba Vanga believed that humanity's ingenuity would play a crucial role in its survival. She predicted that advances in technology, such as the development of artificial food sources and the use of renewable energy, would help mitigate some of the damage caused by environmental collapse. However, she also warned that these innovations would not be enough on their own; they would need to be coupled with a deep shift in human values toward sustainability and cooperation.

A New Beginning or a Final Decline?: Baba Vanga's long apocalypse leaves open the possibility of either renewal or final decline. She suggested that if humanity could learn from its mistakes and embrace a more compassionate, cooperative, and sustainable way of life, it might emerge from the apocalypse stronger and wiser. However, if humanity continues down its current path of materialism, exploitation, and division, the collapse could become irreversible, leading to the eventual extinction of human civilization.

Conclusion: A Slow Descent, But Not Without Hope

Baba Vanga's prophecy of a long, drawn-out apocalypse presents a complex vision of humanity's future—one filled with conflict, environmental decline, technological disruption, and moral decay. Yet, her predictions also offer a glimmer of hope, suggesting that humanity's resilience, ingenuity, and capacity for cooperation could allow it to survive and even thrive in the face of these challenges.

In this chapter, we explored the stages of Baba Vanga's long apocalypse, from the initial conflicts and environmental disasters to humanity's struggle to adapt and find new ways of living. Her prophecy serves as both a warning and a call to action, urging us to reconsider our relationship with the planet, each other, and the technologies we create. While the future she foresaw is filled with uncertainty, Baba Vanga's vision reminds us that survival is possible—if we are willing to learn from our mistakes and change the course of our history.

Faith in Prophecy: The Psychology of Belief in Baba Vanga

Baba Vanga's prophecies have inspired belief and devotion in countless followers, many of whom see her as a figure endowed with supernatural insight into the future. Her predictions—ranging from global disasters to personal revelations—have captivated the imaginations of people around the world. But why do so many place their faith in her prophecies? What is it about her particular brand of mysticism that compels individuals to accept her visions as truth? The psychology of belief in prophecy, particularly in figures like Baba Vanga, is rooted in deep human needs: for guidance, understanding of the unknown, and a sense of control over a chaotic world.

In this chapter, we explore the psychology behind the belief in Baba Vanga's prophecies. We examine the cognitive, emotional, and social factors that contribute to the acceptance of her visions, as well as the powerful role that prophecy plays in providing comfort, purpose, and a framework for understanding the future. Additionally, we consider the ways in which belief in prophecy interacts with skepticism, and why some people are more inclined to believe in mystics like Baba Vanga than others.

The Desire for Certainty in an Uncertain World

At the core of belief in prophecy is the human desire for certainty in an uncertain world. Life is filled with unpredictability—political instability, natural disasters, personal misfortunes—and the future is always unknown. For many, figures like Baba Vanga offer a sense of stability by providing glimpses into what lies ahead. Her prophecies, though sometimes cryptic or metaphorical, are seen as pathways to understanding the future, which in turn reduces the anxiety that comes with uncertainty.

Predictive Certainty: Prophets like Baba Vanga offer a sense of control over the unpredictable. Knowing—or believing to know—what will happen next allows individuals to feel prepared. Her predictions about world events such as wars, natural disasters, and political changes, though often alarming, provide a roadmap for what is to come, giving her followers a sense of preparedness even in the face of uncertainty.

Coping with Fear: Belief in Baba Vanga's prophecies also serves as a coping mechanism for managing fear, particularly fear of the unknown. For many people, the unpredictability of life creates a sense of existential anxiety. By turning to someone who seemingly possesses knowledge of the future, followers can find comfort in the idea that events are unfolding according to a larger plan—whether it's an apocalypse, a revolution, or a technological breakthrough.

Illusion of Control: The desire for control over one's life is a fundamental psychological drive, and belief in prophecy can provide an illusion of control over external events. Even when the prophecies foretell doom or disaster, having knowledge of these events gives followers a sense of power in their ability to anticipate and react. Baba Vanga's predictions provide not only a glimpse into the future but also the belief that individuals can prepare for or influence that future in some way.

Confirmation Bias: Seeing What We Want to See

One of the key psychological mechanisms that fuels belief in prophecy is confirmation bias. This is the tendency for people to interpret new information in a way that confirms their existing beliefs. For Baba Vanga's followers, her prophecies often seem uncannily accurate because they selectively focus on the predictions that align with real-world events while disregarding those that do not come true.

Retrofitting Predictions: Baba Vanga's prophecies are often vague and open to interpretation, which makes them ripe for retrofitting—applying them to events after they have occurred. For instance, her warning about "two steel birds" hitting America has been linked to the September 11 attacks, but this interpretation only emerged after the event. Followers are able to interpret her words in ways that confirm their belief in her prophetic abilities, reinforcing their faith in her visions.

Selective Memory: People tend to remember the predictions that come true (or appear to) while forgetting those that do not. This selective memory creates the illusion that Baba Vanga's prophecies have a high accuracy rate. Her followers focus on the predictions that align with significant events—such as the fall of the Soviet Union or the 2004 tsunami—while ignoring the less accurate or more ambiguous ones.

Ambiguity and Interpretation: The ambiguity of many of Baba Vanga's prophecies allows for flexible interpretation. Vague language and symbolic imagery can be interpreted in multiple ways, which means that different followers can apply her predictions to different events depending on their own experiences or beliefs. This ambiguity strengthens belief, as her prophecies can be molded to fit a variety of circumstances.

The Role of Social Influence in Belief Formation

Belief in prophecy is also heavily influenced by social factors. For many of Baba Vanga's followers, faith in her predictions is not only a personal conviction but also a shared belief within a community. The collective validation of her prophecies through social networks—family, friends, religious groups, or online communities—helps to reinforce and sustain belief.

Group Identity and Shared Belief: People are more likely to adopt and maintain beliefs that are shared by their social group. Within communities that revere Baba Vanga, faith in her prophecies becomes part of group identity. Belief in her abilities is not just an individual conviction but a shared cultural or spiritual practice. Social reinforcement from others who share the same belief strengthens the individual's confidence in her predictions.

Authority and Credibility: Baba Vanga's reputation as a revered mystic, bolstered by the support of political leaders and other influential figures, lends credibility to her prophecies. The endorsement of well-known individuals—such as Bulgarian leader Todor Zhivkov or Soviet officials—has historically contributed to the perception of her as a credible and authoritative figure. People are more likely to believe in prophecies when they come from sources they perceive as trustworthy or powerful.

Emotional Connection and Personal Testimony: Personal experiences and testimonies from those who claim to have had direct encounters with Baba Vanga add an emotional layer to the belief. Stories of her accurately diagnosing illnesses, predicting personal events, or providing comfort to grieving individuals create a narrative that is hard to dispute. These personal connections help to humanize Baba Vanga, making her prophecies feel more tangible and real.

Prophecy as a Tool for Meaning and Purpose

For many, belief in Baba Vanga's prophecies offers more than just a glimpse into the future—it provides a sense of meaning and purpose in life. Her predictions are often framed within a larger narrative about the fate of humanity, offering a way for individuals to understand their place in the world and their role in shaping the future.

Cosmic Significance: Baba Vanga's prophecies suggest that world events are part of a larger cosmic plan, in which individuals play a role. For her followers, this offers a sense of purpose—whether that means preparing for an apocalyptic event, working toward spiritual enlightenment, or simply navigating personal challenges with the knowledge that everything happens for a reason. This cosmic framework provides comfort, particularly in times of crisis or uncertainty.

Moral and Spiritual Guidance: Beyond forecasting events, Baba Vanga's prophecies often contain moral or spiritual lessons. She warned of the dangers of materialism, environmental destruction, and the loss of human compassion. Her predictions serve as calls for change, urging humanity to adopt more sustainable, compassionate, and spiritually fulfilling ways of living. For many, these messages resonate deeply and provide guidance for living a more meaningful life.

The Role of Suffering and Redemption: Baba Vanga's prophecies frequently emphasize the idea that suffering and hardship are part of a larger process of transformation. Her long-drawn-out apocalypse is not an inevitable end but an opportunity for humanity to learn, grow, and ultimately redeem itself. This narrative offers hope even in the face of disaster, allowing her followers to find meaning in suffering and to believe that redemption is possible.

Skepticism and the Limits of Belief

While Baba Vanga's prophecies have inspired fervent belief, they have also attracted significant skepticism. Sceptics question the validity of her predictions, pointing to the lack of verifiable evidence, the vagueness of her language, and the retrospective nature of many interpretations. The tension between belief and skepticism reflects broader societal debates about the role of mysticism and prophecy in a scientific, rational world.

Critical Thinking and Skeptical Inquiry: Sceptics argue that Baba Vanga's prophecies can often be explained by psychological and social phenomena, such as confirmation bias, selective memory, and the human tendency to find patterns in ambiguous information. They emphasize the importance of critical thinking, urging people to question the validity of prophetic claims and to seek out evidence before accepting them as truth.

The Need for Evidence: A key challenge for sceptics is the lack of documented evidence for many of Baba Vanga's most famous predictions. Much of what is attributed to her is based on oral accounts or second-hand reports, making it difficult to verify whether she truly predicted certain events. This absence of concrete evidence makes it easier for sceptics to dismiss her prophecies as folklore or superstition.

The Persistence of Belief: Despite the skepticism, belief in Baba Vanga's prophecies persists, highlighting the powerful role that faith plays in human psychology. For many of her followers, the emotional and spiritual comfort provided by her predictions outweighs the need for empirical evidence. This tension between belief and skepticism is a reminder that faith in prophecy is often more about emotional fulfillment and existential meaning than it is about factual accuracy.

Conclusion: The Power of Prophecy in the Human Experience

Baba Vanga's prophecies continue to inspire belief, even decades after her death, because they tap into deep psychological and emotional needs. Her followers find in her predictions a sense of certainty, comfort, and purpose in a world that often feels chaotic and unpredictable. Whether seen as a spiritual guide, a cosmic prophet, or simply a source of hope, Baba Vanga's legacy endures through the faith of those who believe in her visions.

In this chapter, we explored the psychology of belief in Baba Vanga's prophecies, examining the cognitive, emotional, and social factors that drive faith in her predictions. From confirmation bias to the desire for certainty, her prophecies offer a powerful framework for understanding the future and navigating the complexities of life. While skepticism remains a counterpoint to this faith, the enduring power of prophecy reflects a fundamental aspect of the human experience: the search for meaning, purpose, and a connection to something greater than ourselves.

Baba Vanga and Climate Change: Predictions for a Warming World

One of the most pressing global issues today is climate change, and Baba Vanga's prophecies for the future align eerily with current scientific predictions about the planet's warming climate. Long before climate change became a topic of international debate, Baba Vanga issued dire warnings about the fate of the Earth, foreseeing environmental catastrophes and the gradual deterioration of the planet's ecosystems. Her prophecies touch on rising sea levels, extreme weather events, resource shortages, and the widespread suffering caused by humanity's neglect of the environment.

In this chapter, we explore Baba Vanga's predictions regarding climate change, their relevance in today's world, and the moral and practical implications of her warnings. We will also consider how her environmental prophecies resonate with contemporary discussions about sustainability, the fragility of Earth's ecosystems, and the urgent need for global action.

The Melting of the Polar Ice Caps: Rising Seas and Sinking Cities

One of Baba Vanga's most significant environmental predictions involved the melting of the polar ice caps. She foresaw a future where the rapid thawing of glaciers and ice sheets would lead to catastrophic sea-level rise, flooding coastal cities and forcing mass migrations.

Rising Sea Levels: Baba Vanga warned that the melting of the ice caps would cause a dramatic rise in global sea levels, inundating low-lying regions and coastal cities around the world. This prophecy mirrors contemporary scientific models, which predict that sea levels could rise by as much as one meter by the end of the 21st century if global warming continues unchecked. Major cities, such as New York, Tokyo, and Miami, would be at risk of flooding, and entire island nations could disappear beneath the waves.

Mass Migrations: According to Baba Vanga, the rising seas would force millions of people to flee their homes, creating unprecedented humanitarian crises. Coastal populations would be displaced, leading to mass migrations toward inland regions. This movement of people could strain resources, cause political tensions, and lead to conflicts as nations grapple with the challenges of absorbing large numbers of climate refugees. These predictions resonate with current concerns about how global migration patterns will shift as sea levels rise.

The Loss of Coastal Economies: Baba Vanga also foresaw the economic devastation that would accompany rising sea levels. Coastal economies, particularly those reliant on tourism, fishing, and trade, would collapse as cities and infrastructure are destroyed by floods. The loss of these economic hubs would have ripple effects throughout the global economy, leading to job losses, food shortages, and increased poverty. Her prophecy suggests that humanity's disregard for the environment could have severe and lasting consequences for future generations.

EXTREME WEATHER EVENTS: Nature's Wrath Unleashed

Baba Vanga predicted that the world would face increasingly severe and frequent weather events as a result of climate change. Her prophecies describe a planet besieged by hurricanes, droughts, wildfires, and other natural disasters, all of which would be exacerbated by human activity.

Hurricanes and Storms: According to Baba Vanga, hurricanes and storms would become more frequent and more destructive, especially in coastal regions. This prophecy aligns with current scientific research, which suggests that warmer ocean temperatures and changing atmospheric conditions are likely to lead to stronger and more intense tropical storms. Communities that were once considered safe from such weather events could find themselves increasingly vulnerable.

Droughts and Desertification: Baba Vanga also foresaw widespread droughts and the expansion of deserts as the planet warms. She predicted that once-fertile regions would become arid and barren, leading to agricultural collapse and food shortages. This prophecy is reflected in current concerns about desertification, particularly in parts of Africa, the Middle East, and Asia, where changing rainfall patterns and rising temperatures are already reducing arable land.

Wildfires and Forest Loss: Another key element of Baba Vanga's prophecy involves the increase in wildfires, particularly in forests and grasslands. She warned that wildfires would ravage large swathes of land, destroying ecosystems and contributing to biodiversity loss. Recent years have seen a significant uptick in wildfires, particularly in regions like California, Australia, and the Amazon rainforest, where warming temperatures, droughts, and human activity have created perfect conditions for fire outbreaks. Baba Vanga's prediction highlights the interconnectedness of climate change and environmental degradation.

Resource Scarcity and the Struggle for Survival

As the planet's climate changes, Baba Vanga foresaw that resource scarcity would become one of the greatest challenges facing humanity. She predicted that access to clean water, food, and energy would be increasingly limited, leading to global conflicts over resources and the breakdown of international cooperation.

Water Shortages: One of Baba Vanga's most alarming predictions involved the scarcity of fresh water. She warned that many parts of the world would face severe water shortages as rivers and lakes dry up and aquifers are depleted. This prophecy reflects growing concerns about the global water crisis, with scientists warning that as much as two-thirds of the world's population could experience water scarcity by 2025. Regions that are already vulnerable to drought, such as sub-Saharan Africa, the Middle East, and parts of South Asia, are expected to be hit hardest.

FOOD INSECURITY: Baba Vanga also predicted widespread food shortages as a result of climate change. She foresaw that changing weather patterns, droughts, and the loss of arable land would make it increasingly difficult to grow enough food to support the global population. This prediction aligns with scientific warnings that agricultural systems will face significant disruption in the coming decades, with crop yields expected to decline in many parts of the world. As food becomes scarcer, Baba Vanga warned that competition for resources would intensify, potentially leading to conflict and social unrest.

Energy Crises: In addition to water and food shortages, Baba Vanga predicted that humanity would face a crisis in its energy supply. She foresaw that fossil fuels would become increasingly scarce, leading to energy shortages and economic collapse in many regions. This prophecy mirrors current concerns about the need to transition to renewable energy sources as the world's supply of oil, coal, and natural gas dwindles. Baba Vanga suggested that humanity's failure to develop sustainable energy systems would have devastating consequences for future generations.

The Consequences of Environmental Neglect

Baba Vanga's prophecies about climate change are not just warnings about the physical changes the planet will undergo—they also carry a deeper moral message. She believed that humanity's exploitation of the Earth and disregard for the environment would ultimately lead to its downfall, and that only through a radical shift in values could the planet be saved.

The Cost of Greed and Materialism: Baba Vanga frequently warned that humanity's focus on material wealth and consumption was leading to environmental destruction. She believed that industrialization, deforestation, and pollution were the results of human greed and a failure to respect the natural world. According to her prophecy, the consequences of this exploitation would be catastrophic, with the planet fighting back against the damage done by humanity.

Moral Decline and Environmental Collapse: Baba Vanga saw a connection between moral and environmental decline, predicting that as humans lost touch with their spiritual values, they would become more disconnected from nature. She warned that this moral decay would manifest in environmental destruction, as people prioritized short-term gains over long-term sustainability. Her prophecies serve as a call to action, urging humanity to reconnect with the Earth and adopt more sustainable practices before it is too late.

The Potential for Redemption: Despite her dire warnings, Baba Vanga also foresaw the possibility of redemption. She believed that if humanity could recognize the error of its ways and make a conscious effort to protect the environment, it could avoid the worst of the environmental collapse. Her prophecy suggests that the future is not set in stone, and that the choices made today will determine the fate of future generations.

BABA VANGA'S ENVIRONMENTAL Legacy

Baba Vanga's prophecies about climate change resonate deeply with contemporary environmental concerns. Her warnings about rising sea levels, extreme weather events, and resource shortages align with scientific predictions about the impacts of global warming, and her moral message about humanity's responsibility to the Earth is more relevant than ever.

A Prophet Ahead of Her Time: Baba Vanga's environmental prophecies are remarkable for how closely they align with modern scientific understanding of climate change. Long before climate science gained mainstream attention, she predicted many of the same issues that now dominate global discussions about the future of the planet. Her warnings serve as a reminder that the consequences of climate change are not just theoretical—they are real, and they are happening now.

A Call for Action: Baba Vanga's prophecies offer more than just a glimpse into a dystopian future—they also provide a call to action. Her vision suggests that while the environmental challenges ahead are immense, there is still time to change course. By adopting more sustainable practices, reducing consumption, and working together to protect the planet, humanity can avert the worst of the environmental collapse she foresaw.

Conclusion: Baba Vanga's Vision for a Warming World

Baba Vanga's prophecies about climate change paint a sobering picture of the future, one in which the planet is ravaged by rising seas, extreme weather, and resource shortages. Yet her vision is not without hope. She believed that humanity still has the power to change its fate, and that by adopting a more sustainable and compassionate relationship with the Earth, we can avoid the worst of the environmental disasters she predicted.

In this chapter, we explored Baba Vanga's predictions for a warming world, examining how her prophecies align with current scientific understanding of climate change and the potential consequences for humanity. Her warnings serve as both a prophecy and a moral lesson, urging us to take action before it is too late. As we face an uncertain future, Baba Vanga's vision reminds us that the fate of the planet is in our hands, and that the choices we make today will determine the world we leave for future generations.

Life on Venus: Prophetic or Impossible Dream?

Among Baba Vanga's many intriguing prophecies, one of the most puzzling and ambitious involves the planet Venus. She predicted that by 2028, humanity would begin exploring Venus in search of resources, suggesting that Venus could offer an alternative energy source as Earth's environment deteriorates. The idea of Venus being a viable location for human exploration or even habitation has captivated both believers in her prophecies and those with a curiosity about space exploration. However, Venus is a planet known for its extreme and hostile environment, raising the question: is Baba Vanga's prophecy about life on Venus a prophetic vision of a distant scientific breakthrough, or an impossible dream?

In this chapter, we explore Baba Vanga's prediction of Venus exploration, examining both the scientific challenges and the potential technological advancements that could one day make Venus a site of human exploration. We also consider the broader symbolic meaning of her prophecy and whether her vision could serve as a metaphor for humanity's relentless quest for survival in a world on the brink of environmental collapse.

Venus: The Hellish Neighbor

Venus, the second planet from the Sun, has long fascinated astronomers and scientists, but it is widely regarded as one of the least hospitable planets in the solar system. With surface temperatures hotter than 450°C (842°F), a thick atmosphere composed primarily of carbon dioxide, and clouds of sulfuric acid, Venus presents an extreme and deadly environment. These conditions make the idea of human exploration—and particularly resource extraction or colonization—seem impossible by today's standards.

Extreme Temperatures: Venus is often called Earth's "sister planet" due to its similar size and proximity to the Sun, but the planet's surface is hotter than that of Mercury, even though Mercury is closer to the Sun. The extreme heat on Venus is due to its runaway greenhouse effect, where carbon dioxide traps heat in the atmosphere. With surface temperatures far beyond what humans or current technology can withstand, operating any sort of equipment on Venus presents enormous challenges.

Crushing Atmospheric Pressure: The atmospheric pressure on Venus is about 92 times greater than Earth's, equivalent to the pressure found nearly a mile beneath the ocean. This intense pressure would crush most spacecraft and exploration vehicles not specifically designed for such conditions. The challenge of landing on and exploring Venus requires the development of technology far more advanced than what exists today.

Acidic Atmosphere: Venus' atmosphere is filled with clouds of sulfuric acid, making it highly corrosive. Any exploration vehicles or technologies sent to Venus would need to be resistant to acid corrosion, further complicating the logistics of exploration. This also makes any notion of human presence on the planet seem highly unlikely, as even brief exposure to the atmosphere would be deadly without advanced protection.

Given these conditions, many sceptics view Baba Vanga's prophecy about Venus exploration as scientifically implausible. However, space exploration has often defied expectations, and some researchers believe that with future technological advancements, Venus could still hold potential for exploration.

The Search for Resources on Venus: Is It Possible?

Despite the hostile environment, Baba Vanga's prophecy suggests that Venus could become a source of energy and resources for humanity. This idea is not entirely without merit, as scientists have long speculated about the potential for resource extraction in space, particularly from asteroids, moons, and other planets. While Venus may not be the first choice for resource exploration, its potential should not be dismissed entirely.

Atmospheric Resources: While the surface of Venus is inhospitable, its upper atmosphere presents less extreme conditions. At an altitude of around 50 to 60 kilometers (31 to 37 miles), temperatures and pressures are more similar to Earth's, leading some scientists to speculate about the possibility of airborne colonies or research stations floating in Venus' atmosphere. These stations could potentially extract valuable gases or elements, such as carbon dioxide and nitrogen, which could be used for industrial purposes or even as fuels in the future.

Solar Energy: Venus receives a significant amount of solar radiation due to its proximity to the Sun, making it a potential candidate for solar energy collection. While the thick atmosphere poses challenges, advancements in solar technology might one day allow for the collection of energy in the upper atmosphere or from orbit around Venus. Baba Vanga's prophecy could be interpreted as a vision of humanity harnessing solar power from Venus to solve Earth's energy crisis.

Terraforming and the Long-Term Vision: Some futurists have even speculated about the possibility of terraforming Venus—modifying its environment to make it more Earth-like. While this idea remains highly theoretical, advances in space technology and environmental engineering might one day make it possible to alter the atmospheric composition of Venus, reducing the greenhouse effect and creating a more habitable climate. If humanity ever reaches such a technological level, Venus could become a viable outpost for human civilization.

Space Exploration and Technological Breakthroughs

Baba Vanga's prediction of Venus exploration may also be viewed through the lens of technological breakthroughs that are difficult to envision today but could become reality in the future. Throughout history, humanity has consistently overcome seemingly insurmountable obstacles in its pursuit of exploration and discovery. From landing on the Moon to exploring Mars, space exploration has often defied initial skepticism, and Venus could be the next frontier.

ADVANCES IN SPACECRAFT Design: The current technological limitations that make Venus exploration difficult—extreme temperatures, high pressure, and corrosive atmosphere—might be overcome with future advancements in spacecraft and exploration vehicle design. For example, materials that can withstand high temperatures and pressures are already in development, and next-generation space probes could one day explore Venus for extended periods.

AI and Robotic Exploration: One of the most promising areas for space exploration is the development of artificial intelligence and autonomous robots. In a hostile environment like Venus, where human presence would be extremely dangerous, robotic explorers equipped with AI could conduct extensive research and resource extraction. These robots could withstand the harsh conditions and relay valuable data back to Earth, advancing humanity's understanding of the planet and its potential.

Interplanetary Resource Networks: Baba Vanga's vision of using Venus as a resource hub could align with the broader concept of interplanetary resource networks. As humanity expands its presence in space, planets, moons, and asteroids might be used to supply Earth and other colonies with vital resources. Venus, despite its challenges, could play a role in this network, particularly if advanced technology allows for the extraction of solar energy or atmospheric gases.

The Symbolism of Venus in Baba Vanga's Prophecy

While Baba Vanga's prophecy about Venus could be interpreted as a literal prediction of future space exploration, it may also hold symbolic meaning. Venus has long been associated with love, beauty, and rebirth in mythology and astrology, and Baba Vanga's vision of humanity turning to Venus for resources during a time of environmental collapse on Earth could represent humanity's search for renewal and survival.

Venus as a Metaphor for Rebirth: In many ancient cultures, Venus was viewed as a symbol of life and renewal. Baba Vanga's prediction could be interpreted as a metaphor for humanity's attempt to find new ways of sustaining itself as Earth's environment deteriorates. By turning to Venus, humanity may be symbolically seeking a second chance, a new source of energy and life to replace what has been lost on Earth.

Humanity's Quest for Survival: Baba Vanga's prophecy about Venus aligns with the broader theme of survival that runs through many of her predictions. Faced with environmental collapse, resource depletion, and conflict, humanity must look beyond Earth for solutions. Venus, as one of the most inhospitable planets in the solar system, represents the ultimate challenge—and the ultimate hope—for human survival. The prophecy suggests that humanity's ingenuity and determination will drive exploration and innovation, even in the most extreme circumstances.

SKEPTICISM AND SCIENTIFIC Reality

Despite the imaginative possibilities presented by Baba Vanga's prophecy, many scientists and sceptics remain highly doubtful that Venus could ever serve as a viable destination for human exploration or resource extraction. The planet's extreme conditions make it one of the least likely candidates for human habitation, and significant breakthroughs in space technology would be required before Venus could be explored at the level envisioned in Baba Vanga's prediction.

Scientific Challenges: From the extreme heat to the crushing atmospheric pressure, Venus poses almost insurmountable scientific challenges. Sceptics argue that there are far more promising targets for exploration and resource extraction in the solar system, such as Mars or the moons of Jupiter and Saturn, where conditions are less hostile and more conducive to human presence.

Speculative Technology: While advances in technology may one day allow for limited exploration of Venus, sceptics contend that the idea of resource extraction or colonization remains speculative at best. They argue that Baba Vanga's prophecy, while intriguing, is more likely a reflection of humanity's dreams of space exploration than a realistic prediction of future events.

Conclusion: Prophecy or Impossible Dream?

Baba Vanga's prophecy about life on Venus remains one of her most fascinating and controversial predictions. While the extreme conditions on Venus make exploration seem unlikely by today's standards, future technological advancements could open new possibilities for space exploration and resource extraction. Whether her vision was truly prophetic or simply an impossible dream, Baba Vanga's prediction serves as a reminder of humanity's relentless pursuit of survival and discovery, even in the face of overwhelming challenges.

In this chapter, we examined the scientific and symbolic aspects of Baba Vanga's prophecy about Venus exploration. While skepticism persists, her vision taps into the broader human desire to explore the unknown and find solutions to the existential threats facing our planet. As space exploration continues to advance, perhaps one day humanity will look to Venus—not just as a symbol of survival, but as a destination for innovation and hope.

The Global Spread of Communism: Baba Vanga's Vision of a Political Future

---

Baba Vanga's prophecies often touched on geopolitical and social shifts, foreseeing major events that would reshape the political landscape. One of her most intriguing and controversial predictions was the global return of communism by the year 2076. According to her vision, communism would spread not just in former Soviet states or Eastern Europe but would extend across the entire world. In a time when capitalism dominates the global economy, and many associate communism with the Cold War and its eventual collapse in the late 20th century, Baba Vanga's prediction raises questions: Could communism make a global comeback? And if so, what would that future look like?

In this chapter, we delve into Baba Vanga's prophecy about the global spread of communism, exploring both the historical context and the current global trends that might lend weight to her prediction. We will also examine how her vision might be interpreted—whether as a literal return of Marxist ideology or as a symbolic shift toward more egalitarian, collective systems in response to the failures of unchecked capitalism.

The Historical Context of Communism

To understand Baba Vanga's prophecy about the future spread of communism, we must first explore its historical context. Communism, as an ideology, originated with Karl Marx and Friedrich Engels in the 19th century, who envisioned a classless, stateless society where the means of production were owned collectively, and wealth was distributed equally. This vision sharply contrasted with capitalism, which Marx and Engels saw as exploitative and unjust, with wealth concentrated in the hands of a few.

The Soviet Union and the Spread of Communism: The Russian Revolution of 1917 marked the birth of the first major communist state—the Soviet Union—under the leadership of Vladimir Lenin. Throughout much of the 20th century, communism spread to other parts of the world, particularly in Eastern Europe, China, Cuba, and parts of Southeast Asia. The Cold War, which dominated international relations in the mid-20th century, was largely a struggle between the capitalist West, led by the United States, and the communist East, led by the Soviet Union.

The Collapse of Communism in the Late 20th Century: Despite its early spread, communism began to falter by the late 20th century. The Soviet Union collapsed in 1991, and many former communist states transitioned to market economies. In China, while the Communist Party remained in power, the country embraced market reforms that allowed capitalism to flourish. For many, the fall of the Soviet Union marked the "end of history"—a belief that capitalism and liberal democracy would become the dominant global systems.

Given this history, Baba Vanga's prophecy of a global return to communism by 2076 seems to run counter to current trends. However, it is possible that her vision reflects a deeper understanding of political and social cycles, predicting a response to the shortcomings of modern capitalism.

The Failures of Capitalism: Seeds of Revolution?

While capitalism has brought economic growth and technological advancement to much of the world, it has also created significant challenges—rising inequality, environmental destruction, and political instability. Baba Vanga's prophecy of a global return to communism could be seen as a response to these failures, predicting that the flaws of capitalism will eventually drive people toward alternative political systems.

Economic Inequality: One of the key criticisms of capitalism is the widening gap between the rich and the poor. While the global economy has grown, wealth has increasingly concentrated in the hands of a small elite. This inequality has sparked movements for social and economic justice, with calls for policies like wealth redistribution, universal healthcare, and a guaranteed basic income. Baba Vanga's prophecy could be interpreted as foreseeing a world in which these movements gain traction, leading to a political shift toward collectivism and the redistribution of resources.

Environmental Crisis: Another major challenge of capitalism is its impact on the environment. The profit-driven nature of capitalist economies often prioritizes short-term gains over long-term sustainability, contributing to environmental degradation, climate change, and resource depletion. Baba Vanga's vision of a communist future might reflect a world in which humanity is forced to adopt more collective, sustainable systems to address these crises. Communism, with its focus on shared resources and centralized planning, could offer an alternative model for managing global resources and protecting the environment.

Political Discontent and Social Movements: In recent years, many countries have seen a rise in populist and anti-establishment movements, fueled by dissatisfaction with the political and economic status quo. From the Occupy Wall Street protests to the rise of democratic socialism in the United States and Europe, there is a growing demand for alternatives to neoliberal capitalism. Baba Vanga's prediction could be viewed as a reflection of these shifting political dynamics, suggesting that by 2076, these movements could coalesce into a new global political order.

The Global Spread of Communism: Literal or Symbolic?

When interpreting Baba Vanga's prophecy about the return of global communism, it's important to consider whether her vision should be taken literally or symbolically. While a literal return of Marxist-Leninist communism seems unlikely given the current geopolitical landscape, her prophecy may instead point to a broader shift toward more collective and egalitarian systems.

A Return to Marxist Ideology?: In the most literal sense, Baba Vanga's prophecy suggests that communism, as envisioned by Marx and Engels, will make a comeback and spread across the globe. This would involve the overthrow of capitalist systems, the abolition of private property, and the establishment of a classless society. While this vision seems improbable given the dominance of capitalism today, it's possible that social and economic crises in the coming decades could create the conditions for revolutionary change.

The Rise of Democratic Socialism or Hybrid Systems: A more plausible interpretation of Baba Vanga's prophecy is that she foresaw the rise of democratic socialism or hybrid political systems that combine elements of socialism and capitalism. Democratic socialism advocates for the collective ownership of key industries (such as healthcare, education, and energy) while maintaining democratic political institutions. This system seeks to address the inequalities of capitalism while preserving individual freedoms, and it has gained popularity in parts of Europe and the United States. Baba Vanga's vision could point to a future where such systems become the global norm, representing a compromise between capitalism and communism.

A Symbolic Shift Toward Cooperation and Collectivism: Another interpretation of Baba Vanga's prophecy is that it represents a symbolic shift away from hyper-individualism and competition toward a more cooperative, collective approach to global challenges. In a world facing climate change, resource scarcity, and political instability, humanity may be forced to adopt new systems of governance that prioritize the common good over individual profit. This shift might not involve communism in the traditional sense but could instead reflect a new form of global governance that emphasizes collective action, social welfare, and environmental sustainability.

Technological Advancements and the Future of Work

Another factor that could drive the return of communism—or at least a more collective approach to economic systems—is the rise of automation and artificial intelligence. As technology advances, many jobs traditionally performed by humans will be automated, potentially leading to widespread unemployment and economic disruption. Baba Vanga's prophecy may reflect a future in which these technological changes force a reevaluation of how wealth is distributed and how society functions.

Automation and Unemployment: As robots and AI take over jobs in manufacturing, service industries, and even knowledge work, millions of people could find themselves without traditional employment. In such a scenario, a capitalist system that relies on wage labor may no longer be sustainable. Baba Vanga's vision of a return to communism could represent a world in which automation leads to a more collective approach to wealth distribution, such as universal basic income or state-provided services.

The End of Work as We Know It: Some futurists predict that automation could lead to the end of traditional work, freeing people from the need to labor for survival. In such a world, wealth and resources would need to be distributed collectively, as individuals would no longer earn wages through employment. This post-work society could resemble a form of communism, where resources are owned and distributed by the community rather than concentrated in the hands of a few.

Communism and Global Governance

Baba Vanga's prediction of global communism by 2076 also raises questions about the future of global governance. In a world facing increasingly interconnected challenges—such as climate change, pandemics, and economic inequality—there may be a growing need for collective, international solutions. Her prophecy could point to a future where nations cooperate more closely, or even merge into larger political entities, to address these global problems.

A Global Political Order: Baba Vanga's vision of a worldwide communist system could be interpreted as a prediction of greater global integration. In the face of environmental collapse and resource scarcity, individual nations may be unable to address these challenges on their own. This could lead to the formation of global governance structures that prioritize collective action and resource sharing, moving the world toward a more unified, cooperative political system.

Global Wealth Redistribution: Another possible interpretation of Baba Vanga's prophecy is the rise of global wealth redistribution. In response to rising inequality and the concentration of wealth in a small number of countries and corporations, there could be increasing pressure for international policies that redistribute wealth more equitably across the globe. This could take the form of global taxes on corporations, international aid programs, or even a global basic income system.

Conclusion: A Prophetic Vision of the Future or a Symbolic Warning?

Baba Vanga's prophecy of the global return of communism by 2076 is both fascinating and controversial. While a literal return to Marxist-Leninist communism seems unlikely in today's world, her vision may instead reflect a broader shift toward more egalitarian, collective systems in response to the failures of capitalism. Whether through democratic socialism, hybrid economic models, or symbolic cooperation on a global scale, Baba Vanga's prophecy suggests that humanity will need to find new ways of organizing itself to survive the challenges of the future.

In this chapter, we explored Baba Vanga's vision of global communism, examining the historical context, the current failures of capitalism, and the potential for technological and political changes to drive a shift toward collective governance. Whether seen as a literal prediction or a symbolic warning, Baba Vanga's prophecy serves as a reminder that political and economic systems are not static, and that the future may bring radical changes to the way we live, work, and share resources on a global scale.

Alien Diplomacy or War: Baba Vanga's Speculation on Extraterrestrial Contact

Among Baba Vanga's most intriguing and far-reaching prophecies is her prediction of extraterrestrial contact. According to her vision, by the year 2130, humanity will establish communication with intelligent beings from other planets. This encounter with extraterrestrial civilizations, however, presents a paradox: will it lead to a new era of peaceful cooperation and knowledge exchange, or will it spiral into a devastating interplanetary conflict? Baba Vanga's prophecy leaves open the possibility of both outcomes—either diplomacy or war—and, as we consider the implications of such a monumental event, it is worth exploring both scenarios.

In this chapter, we delve into Baba Vanga's speculation on extraterrestrial contact, examining the historical context of humanity's fascination with alien life, the potential consequences of meeting advanced civilizations, and the technological, political, and ethical challenges that such an encounter would raise. Whether the future brings alien diplomacy or war, Baba Vanga's vision encourages us to reflect on humanity's readiness for contact with life beyond Earth.

The Prophecy: Alien Contact in 2130

Baba Vanga's prophecy about extraterrestrial contact is one of her boldest and most speculative predictions. She foresaw that by 2130, humanity would not only make contact with alien civilizations but would begin to engage in complex relationships with them. Her vision raises fundamental questions about how humanity might react to such an event and how this contact could reshape our understanding of the universe and our place within it.

Establishing Contact: Baba Vanga predicted that contact with extraterrestrial beings would not be a simple, one-time event, but rather the beginning of an ongoing relationship between species. This contact would likely be initiated through advanced communication technologies or space exploration, as humans and aliens develop the ability to reach across the vast distances of space to share knowledge and resources.

A New Era of Cooperation or Conflict?: While the initial contact might be peaceful, Baba Vanga left open the possibility that humanity's interaction with alien civilizations could go in one of two directions: diplomacy or war. In the optimistic version of her prophecy, humans and extraterrestrials would collaborate to solve global problems, share technological advancements, and explore the cosmos together. However, she also warned of the potential for conflict, particularly if humans approached these new beings with fear, aggression, or a desire for domination.

The Search for Extraterrestrial Life: Historical and Scientific Context

The idea of contact with alien civilizations has long fascinated humanity, and Baba Vanga's prophecy reflects a broader cultural and scientific interest in the possibility of life beyond Earth. Throughout history, people have speculated about the existence of extraterrestrials, with philosophical, religious, and scientific perspectives all contributing to the debate.

The Fermi Paradox: One of the most famous scientific discussions surrounding the possibility of alien life is the Fermi Paradox, which asks, "If intelligent extraterrestrial life exists, why haven't we found it yet?" Despite the vastness of the universe and the probability that life could exist elsewhere, humanity has yet to detect definitive evidence of aliens. Baba Vanga's prediction, however, suggests that this will change in the 22nd century, as advancements in space exploration and communication lead to contact with extraterrestrials.

SETI and the Search for Signals: Scientists have been actively searching for extraterrestrial life for decades, particularly through efforts like the Search for Extraterrestrial Intelligence (SETI). These programs scan the cosmos for radio signals or other forms of communication that might indicate the presence of intelligent life. Baba Vanga's vision aligns with this scientific pursuit, suggesting that one day, humanity's efforts to reach out to the stars will bear fruit.

Space Exploration and Technological Breakthroughs: Humanity's exploration of space, particularly through missions to Mars, the moons of Jupiter and Saturn, and beyond, has raised hopes that we might one day find microbial life or evidence of past civilizations. Baba Vanga's prophecy suggests that by 2130, space exploration will have advanced significantly, allowing humans to travel further into space and perhaps make contact with civilizations much older and more technologically advanced than our own.

Alien Diplomacy: A New Era of Cooperation

One possible outcome of Baba Vanga's prophecy is that contact with extraterrestrials will lead to a new era of peaceful cooperation and collaboration. In this scenario, humanity and alien civilizations would work together to solve shared problems, exchange knowledge, and explore the universe.

Technological Exchange: One of the most exciting prospects of alien diplomacy is the potential for a vast exchange of technology and knowledge. Advanced extraterrestrial civilizations could offer solutions to some of humanity's most pressing problems, such as climate change, energy shortages, and disease. In return, humanity could share its own technological and scientific advancements, fostering a mutually beneficial relationship.

Cultural Exchange and New Philosophies: Beyond technology, alien contact could lead to profound cultural and philosophical exchanges. Humans could learn from the experiences of alien civilizations that may have existed for millennia, gaining new insights into morality, governance, art, and spirituality. Such an exchange could spark a renaissance of ideas on Earth, as humans adopt new ways of thinking and living.

A United Humanity: Contact with intelligent life beyond Earth could also serve as a unifying force for humanity. The realization that we are not alone in the universe might encourage nations to work together, setting aside their differences in the face of a common challenge. This cooperation could lead to the formation of a global government or coalition dedicated to managing relations with extraterrestrial species and ensuring the survival of both humanity and our alien counterparts.

Alien Conflict: The Possibility of Interplanetary War

While the idea of peaceful collaboration with extraterrestrials is an appealing one, Baba Vanga's prophecy also suggests the possibility of conflict. History shows that encounters between different civilizations—particularly when one is more technologically advanced than the other—often lead to war, colonization, or exploitation. Could the same fate befall humanity if we come into contact with extraterrestrials?

Fear and Miscommunication: One of the greatest risks of alien contact is the potential for miscommunication or misunderstanding. Differences in language, culture, or biology could lead to unintended hostility. Humans, driven by fear of the unknown, might react aggressively to extraterrestrials, triggering a conflict that could escalate into war. Alternatively, extraterrestrials might see humanity as a threat to their own survival and take preemptive action to neutralize that threat.

Competition for Resources: Another potential source of conflict is competition for resources. If extraterrestrials require the same resources as humans—such as water, minerals, or energy sources—this could lead to tension and even interplanetary war. Baba Vanga's prophecy suggests that humanity's future interactions with aliens may not be purely diplomatic, and the scramble for valuable resources could drive both sides into conflict.

Technological Disparity: If extraterrestrials are significantly more advanced than humanity, the imbalance in technology could lead to a power struggle. Historically, encounters between civilizations with unequal levels of technological development have often resulted in conquest or domination. Baba Vanga's warning about the potential for alien war could reflect the fear that humanity's relatively primitive technology may make us vulnerable to exploitation or control by more advanced alien species.

The Ethics of Alien Contact: How Should Humanity Respond?

Baba Vanga's prophecy raises important ethical questions about how humanity should respond to the discovery of intelligent extraterrestrial life. Whether the encounter leads to diplomacy or conflict, humanity must grapple with the moral implications of interacting with an entirely new form of life.

Rights and Recognition for Alien Beings: If humanity makes contact with extraterrestrial civilizations, we will need to decide how to treat these beings. Do they have the same rights as humans? Should we extend the protections of human rights to non-human, intelligent species? Baba Vanga's prophecy suggests that humanity's response to alien life will test our ethical frameworks and force us to reconsider what it means to be sentient and deserving of respect.

Peaceful First Contact: To avoid conflict, it will be essential to approach alien contact with diplomacy and caution. Establishing peaceful communication channels, ensuring mutual respect, and avoiding actions that could be perceived as threats will be key to ensuring that the encounter remains peaceful. Baba Vanga's prophecy of possible war serves as a reminder of the dangers of fear and aggression, urging humanity to seek diplomacy first.

The Risks of Exploitation: Just as humanity has a history of exploiting natural resources and weaker civilizations, there is a risk that extraterrestrial contact could lead to exploitation—either by us or by them. Baba Vanga's vision suggests that alien contact could mirror human colonialism, with one civilization attempting to dominate or exploit the other for resources or knowledge. Ethical guidelines for interplanetary relations will need to be developed to prevent such exploitation.

Conclusion: Diplomacy, War, or Both?

Baba Vanga's prophecy about alien contact leaves us with two possible futures—one of peaceful diplomacy and cooperation, and the other of devastating conflict. Whether humanity's first contact with extraterrestrials leads to war or collaboration will depend on how we approach the encounter, how we interpret the intentions of alien civilizations, and how we manage our own fears and ambitions.

In this chapter, we explored the potential outcomes of extraterrestrial contact, from technological and cultural exchange to interplanetary conflict. Baba Vanga's vision serves as both a warning and an opportunity, reminding us that humanity's future is not set in stone. Whether we rise to the occasion and establish peaceful relations with alien species or fall into the trap of fear and aggression will determine the course of history—not just for humanity, but for all intelligent life in the universe.

The Evacuation of Earth: What the Future Holds

One of Baba Vanga's most haunting and apocalyptic prophecies involves the evacuation of Earth. According to her vision, by the year 3797, humanity will be forced to leave Earth as it becomes uninhabitable due to environmental collapse, technological failures, or some other catastrophic event. This prophecy paints a stark picture of the future, where Earth, once humanity's cradle, can no longer sustain life. Whether through environmental destruction, resource depletion, or the fallout from interstellar conflict, Baba Vanga suggests that humanity's survival will ultimately depend on finding a new home in the cosmos.

In this chapter, we explore Baba Vanga's prediction of Earth's evacuation, examining the potential causes that could lead to such a drastic outcome, the scientific efforts to make interplanetary migration a reality, and the moral and ethical questions raised by the prospect of abandoning our home planet. While the idea of evacuating Earth may seem distant and speculative, the warning embedded in Baba Vanga's prophecy encourages us to reflect on the actions we take today and their long-term consequences for future generations.

The Prophecy: Earth's Final Days in 3797

Baba Vanga's prophecy of Earth's evacuation offers a chilling glimpse into the far future. In her vision, by 3797, Earth will no longer be capable of supporting human life. Whether due to environmental degradation, resource exhaustion, or a cosmic disaster, the only option for humanity will be to leave the planet and seek refuge elsewhere in the universe.

The Uninhabitable Earth: Baba Vanga foresaw that by this distant future, Earth's ecosystems would collapse entirely, making the planet uninhabitable for all forms of life. This prediction raises questions about what specific events might lead to such a dire outcome. Could it be runaway climate change, nuclear war, a catastrophic asteroid impact, or some unforeseen disaster? Baba Vanga leaves the exact cause open to interpretation, but the urgency of her vision remains clear—humans must find a way to escape Earth's fate.

The Search for a New Home: According to Baba Vanga, the evacuation of Earth will be humanity's last hope for survival. As Earth deteriorates, humans will embark on an interstellar journey to find a new planet that can sustain life. This prophecy taps into humanity's long-standing fascination with space exploration and the idea of colonizing other planets as a means of securing the future of the species.

Environmental Collapse: A Slow-Motion Apocalypse

One of the most plausible scenarios for the evacuation of Earth involves the gradual collapse of the planet's ecosystems. Baba Vanga's prophecy aligns with growing scientific concerns about climate change, resource depletion, and environmental degradation, all of which could contribute to a future where Earth becomes uninhabitable.

Runaway Climate Change: Climate change is already transforming Earth's environment, leading to rising temperatures, melting ice caps, and more extreme weather events. If left unchecked, this warming trend could trigger a series of irreversible changes—such as the release of methane from permafrost, the collapse of critical ecosystems, and the disruption of global food and water supplies—that would make large portions of the planet uninhabitable.

Mass Extinctions and Ecosystem Collapse: The loss of biodiversity and the collapse of ecosystems are other potential drivers of Earth's uninhabitability. As more species go extinct and ecosystems fail, the services they provide—such as pollination, oxygen production, and carbon sequestration—will diminish, further destabilizing the planet's ability to support human life. Baba Vanga's vision of Earth's final days could be the culmination of centuries of environmental neglect.

Resource Depletion: Another contributing factor to Earth's decline could be the depletion of essential resources, such as fresh water, arable land, and energy sources. As populations grow and demand increases, humanity could exhaust the planet's resources, leaving future generations without the means to survive on Earth.

Technological Failures and Global Catastrophe

In addition to environmental collapse, Baba Vanga's prophecy may also reflect the possibility of technological failures or catastrophic events that could render Earth uninhabitable. As humanity becomes increasingly reliant on technology, the risks associated with its failure become more pronounced.

Nuclear War: One of the most devastating scenarios for Earth's future is the possibility of nuclear war. A full-scale nuclear conflict could cause widespread destruction, triggering a nuclear winter that blocks sunlight, cools the planet, and disrupts global agriculture. In such a scenario, the fallout from nuclear explosions and radiation would make large parts of Earth uninhabitable for centuries.

Artificial Intelligence and Technological Risk: Another possible cause of Earth's uninhabitability could be the rise of artificial intelligence (AI) and advanced technologies that spiral out of human control. Some futurists and scientists have warned that AI, if improperly managed, could pose existential risks to humanity. Baba Vanga's prophecy may hint at the dangers of over-reliance on technology or the unintended consequences of technological advancement.

Cosmic Disasters: In addition to human-caused disasters, Baba Vanga's prophecy could also reflect the possibility of cosmic events, such as asteroid impacts, solar flares, or supernova explosions, that could devastate Earth's environment. While such events are rare, they are not impossible, and scientists have long recognized the potential for catastrophic space-based disasters.

The Science of Space Colonization: Preparing for Humanity's Escape

Baba Vanga's vision of Earth's evacuation aligns with ongoing scientific efforts to explore the possibility of interplanetary colonization. While the idea of escaping Earth may seem like science fiction, advances in space exploration, robotics, and artificial intelligence are bringing the prospect of human settlements on other planets closer to reality.

Mars Colonization: One of the most likely candidates for humanity's future home is Mars. Several space agencies, including NASA and private companies like SpaceX, are working on plans to send humans to Mars and establish permanent colonies there. Mars offers some advantages for colonization, including a day-length similar to Earth's and the presence of water ice. However, its thin atmosphere, lack of magnetic field, and harsh surface conditions present significant challenges.

Terraforming and Planetary Engineering: One potential way to make other planets habitable is through terraforming—modifying a planet's atmosphere, temperature, and surface to support human life. While this concept remains speculative, some scientists believe that it might be possible to transform Mars, Venus, or other celestial bodies into environments more suitable for human habitation. Baba Vanga's prophecy suggests that humanity may need to develop such technologies to survive beyond Earth.

Interstellar Travel and Habitable Exoplanets: Another avenue of exploration is the search for habitable exoplanets—planets outside our solar system that could support life. Astronomers have already discovered thousands of exoplanets, some of which lie in the "habitable zone" of their stars, where conditions may allow for liquid water. While interstellar travel presents immense challenges, advances in propulsion technology, such as nuclear fusion or warp drives, could one day make journeys to distant star systems possible.

Ethical and Moral Questions of Abandoning Earth

The prospect of evacuating Earth raises profound ethical and moral questions. If Earth becomes uninhabitable, who will be chosen to leave, and who will be left behind? How should humanity approach the responsibility of preserving life on Earth versus the need to secure survival elsewhere? Baba Vanga's prophecy forces us to confront these difficult questions.

Who Gets to Leave?: In the event of an evacuation, resources for interplanetary travel will likely be limited. This raises the question of who gets to leave Earth and who must remain behind. Will decisions be based on wealth, social status, or skills? Will it be a lottery system, or will governments choose who is deemed worthy of survival? Baba Vanga's prophecy warns of the potential for inequality and injustice in the face of global disaster.

The Ethics of Abandoning Earth: Another question raised by Baba Vanga's prophecy is whether humanity has the right to abandon Earth altogether. Should efforts to colonize other planets be prioritized over efforts to repair and restore Earth's environment? For some, the idea of abandoning Earth represents a failure to take responsibility for the damage humans have caused to the planet. Baba Vanga's vision suggests that humanity's future may depend on finding a balance between preserving Earth and preparing for the possibility that it cannot be saved.

Preserving Human Culture and Legacy: If humanity must leave Earth, what aspects of human culture, history, and knowledge should be preserved? Baba Vanga's prophecy hints at the end of an era for humanity, but it also raises the possibility of starting anew on a distant planet. As humans venture into space, they will need to decide what elements of their past to carry with them and what new legacies to build in the future.

Conclusion: The Final Exodus or a New Beginning?

Baba Vanga's prophecy of Earth's evacuation paints a grim picture of humanity's future, where the planet we call home is no longer capable of sustaining life. Yet, her vision also suggests the potential for a new beginning. As humans venture into space in search of new homes, they carry with them not only the knowledge of Earth's failures but also the hope of building a better future on distant worlds.

In this chapter, we explored the possible causes of Earth's uninhabitability, from environmental collapse to technological failures and cosmic disasters. We also examined the scientific efforts to make interplanetary migration a reality, as well as the ethical questions raised by the prospect of abandoning Earth. Baba Vanga's prophecy serves as both a warning and an inspiration, reminding us that while the future may hold great challenges, it also offers opportunities for survival, exploration, and renewal beyond the stars.

As we look to the future, the evacuation of Earth may one day become a necessity—but it also represents humanity's enduring drive to survive, adapt, and explore the unknown. Whether it is Mars, another planet, or even a distant star system, Baba Vanga's vision suggests that humanity's journey is far from over. The cosmos awaits, and the future holds both danger and hope.

Prophetic Shadows: Baba Vanga's Mysterious Methods

Baba Vanga, known for her astonishing predictions and spiritual foresight, remains a figure of fascination largely due to the mysterious methods behind her prophecies. Despite her blindness, she claimed to possess extraordinary abilities that enabled her to foresee future events with startling accuracy. But how exactly did Baba Vanga receive her visions? Her methods, which seemed to defy the conventional understanding of time and knowledge, remain an enigma. They blended elements of mysticism, spirituality, and Balkan folklore, creating a process that is as cryptic as her predictions themselves.

In this chapter, we explore the elusive and intriguing techniques Baba Vanga used to access the future. We delve into the sources of her visions, the rituals she performed, and the belief systems that influenced her prophetic abilities. By examining the shadowy and symbolic nature of her methods, we uncover how she became one of the most revered mystics of the 20th century.

The Origins of Her Gift: Tragedy and Spiritual Awakening

The roots of Baba Vanga's prophetic abilities are often traced back to the life-changing event that occurred when she was just 12 years old. A severe storm swept her off her feet, leaving her injured and, ultimately, blind. This traumatic event is said to have opened a new dimension of perception for her, transforming her from an ordinary girl into a mystic with extraordinary gifts.

The Awakening of Her Abilities: Baba Vanga often described her blindness as the catalyst that unlocked her prophetic abilities. According to her, losing her sight enhanced her connection to the unseen world, allowing her to access information that was hidden from ordinary senses. Many people believed that her blindness heightened her sensitivity to spiritual forces, which she claimed provided her with insight into both the personal lives of those who sought her advice and the future of the world itself.

Spiritual Forces and Communication: Baba Vanga attributed her visions to communication with spiritual entities. She claimed that invisible beings, which she described as "creatures of light," guided her and passed on information about the future. This spiritual connection was central to her prophetic process, making her not just a fortune teller but a medium between the material world and the divine.

The Role of Rituals and Objects in Her Prophetic Practice

Baba Vanga's methods of prophecy involved a number of rituals that drew upon her deep connection to the natural world and her belief in spiritual energies. Her sessions with clients often involved physical objects, water, or other mediums that helped her "see" into the future.

THE USE OF WATER AS a Medium: One of the most fascinating elements of Baba Vanga's practice was her use of water as a conduit for her visions. She would ask her clients to bring water from a specific source, such as a natural spring or river, which she believed carried spiritual energy. By touching or holding the water, Baba Vanga would enter a trance-like state, allowing her to receive visions about the person's future or current circumstances. Water, to Baba Vanga, was more than just a physical substance—it was a bridge to the spiritual realm.

Personal Objects and Energy Imprints: In addition to water, Baba Vanga often requested personal items from her clients, such as a piece of jewelry or clothing. She believed that these objects contained the energetic imprint of the person who owned them, and by holding the item, she could connect to that individual's past, present, and future. This practice is akin to psychometry, a form of divination where a person reads the energy of objects to gain insights about their owner.

Trance and Meditation: Baba Vanga's prophecies were typically delivered while she was in a deep, meditative state. She would close her eyes and focus on the energy around her, often losing awareness of her surroundings as she received information from the spiritual realm. During these trance-like moments, Baba Vanga claimed to see vivid images and symbols that would guide her predictions.

The Symbolism of Her Visions

Baba Vanga's prophecies were often cryptic, filled with metaphors and symbolic imagery that required interpretation. Unlike straightforward predictions, her visions were deeply metaphorical, and their true meaning often became clear only after the events had taken place.

The Use of Metaphor: Many of Baba Vanga's prophecies were expressed in symbolic terms. For example, her famous prediction about the September 11 attacks referred to "two steel birds" crashing into buildings, a metaphor for the airplanes that hit the World Trade Center towers. Such metaphors added a layer of mystery to her predictions and required those who heard them to reflect deeply on their potential meanings.

Visions of Distant Futures: Baba Vanga often predicted events far beyond her own lifetime, offering glimpses of what the world might look like centuries or millennia into the future. Her long-range prophecies—such as the melting of the polar ice caps or the evacuation of Earth—demonstrated her ability to tap into a temporal realm that extended far beyond the present. This expansive view of time contributed to the mystical quality of her predictions.

The Influence of Balkan Mysticism and Folk Traditions

Baba Vanga's methods were deeply rooted in the spiritual and mystical traditions of the Balkans, where folk magic, healing practices, and divination were long part of the cultural fabric. These influences shaped her approach to prophecy and informed her belief in the interconnectedness of the physical and spiritual worlds.

Balkan Folk Beliefs: The Balkan region has a rich history of mysticism, blending Christian, pagan, and folk traditions into a unique spiritual landscape. Baba Vanga's methods drew from this blend, incorporating elements of folk magic, healing practices, and religious symbolism. Her use of water and personal objects as mediums for prophecy reflected the importance of natural elements and personal energy in Balkan mysticism.

A Spiritual Healer: In addition to being a prophet, Baba Vanga was also regarded as a healer, offering spiritual guidance and remedies to those in need. She often provided herbal treatments and rituals designed to heal physical ailments or bring peace to troubled individuals. Her role as both a seer and healer made her a trusted figure in her community, and she was sought after for both her prophecies and her spiritual remedies.

Belief, Skepticism, and the Mystery of Her Abilities

Despite her fame, Baba Vanga's prophetic abilities have always been surrounded by debate. While many view her as a genuine mystic with a divine gift, others remain skeptical, questioning the methods and accuracy of her predictions. The mystery surrounding her abilities continues to fuel both fascination and skepticism.

The Role of Suggestion and Interpretation: Critics argue that Baba Vanga's prophecies were often vague and open to interpretation, allowing people to retroactively fit her predictions to actual events. This phenomenon, known as the "Barnum effect," occurs when individuals find personal meaning in general statements. Her predictions about major world events, such as wars or natural disasters, were often interpreted after the fact to match real occurrences.

The Mystery of Her Prophetic Process: Despite the skepticism, Baba Vanga's abilities remain a subject of intrigue. Her unique methods, involving water, personal objects, and trance states, suggest a deep connection to mystical traditions that defy easy explanation. Even those who question the supernatural nature of her prophecies are often struck by the vividness and specificity of some of her predictions.

Conclusion: The Shadowy Legacy of Baba Vanga's Methods

Baba Vanga's prophetic methods remain as mysterious as the visions she shared with the world. Her ability to access the future through ritual, spiritual communication, and symbolic insight set her apart as one of the most fascinating mystics of the 20th century. Whether viewed as a spiritual gift or a product of suggestion and interpretation, Baba Vanga's methods continue to captivate believers and sceptics alike.

In this chapter, we explored the enigmatic techniques Baba Vanga used to make her prophecies, from the use of water as a spiritual medium to the trance-like states in which she delivered her predictions. Her methods, shaped by the cultural and mystical traditions of the Balkans, reflect a complex and multifaceted approach to understanding the future. As we look back on her legacy, the mystery of Baba Vanga's methods remains one of the most enduring aspects of her story—a testament to the power of mysticism and the human desire to glimpse the unknown.

Baba Vanga's Place in History: A Legacy of Mysticism and Prophecy

Baba Vanga stands as one of the most enigmatic and revered figures in modern mysticism. Born in the early 20th century in a small village in the Balkans, she transcended her humble beginnings and the limitations of blindness to become a globally recognized prophet. Throughout her life, she made predictions about world events, natural disasters, technological advancements, and humanity's ultimate fate, touching on both the immediate and the distant future. Whether viewed as a true visionary or a controversial figure, Baba Vanga's legacy continues to influence popular culture, spiritual beliefs, and discussions around prophecy.

In this final chapter, we explore Baba Vanga's place in history, examining how her life and prophecies shaped the modern understanding of mysticism. We will also reflect on her impact on both believers and sceptics, the cultural significance of her predictions, and the lasting influence she has on those seeking to understand the future. As we consider her legacy, we see that Baba Vanga's role as a prophet goes beyond the accuracy of her predictions; it speaks to a deeper human desire to find meaning and insight in an unpredictable world.

Baba Vanga: A Prophet for the Modern Age

While many mystics and prophets are tied to ancient traditions, Baba Vanga's prophecies resonate with the complexities of the modern world. Born in 1911, she lived through some of the most tumultuous times in recent history, including two world wars, the rise and fall of communism, and rapid technological advancements. Her predictions often reflected the fears and anxieties of a world undergoing rapid change.

Predictions in Times of Global Unrest: Baba Vanga's life coincided with a century of global unrest, political upheaval, and shifting ideologies. From the Cold War to the economic crises of the late 20th century, her prophecies often touched on themes of conflict, revolution, and societal transformation. This made her a relevant and timely figure for many who sought her counsel during periods of uncertainty.

A Voice for the Marginalized: Despite her fame, Baba Vanga remained grounded in her rural roots, often speaking on behalf of ordinary people and warning about the dangers of greed, corruption, and environmental degradation. Her prophecies often expressed a concern for the marginalized, predicting the rise of social movements that would challenge the status quo. In this sense, Baba Vanga became a prophet for those seeking change in a world dominated by powerful elites.

Modern Mysticism and Technology: In a world increasingly shaped by technology, Baba Vanga's predictions about artificial intelligence, space exploration, and extraterrestrial contact positioned her as a prophet for the digital age. Her foresight into the potential dangers and benefits of technological advancement resonated with contemporary concerns about the future of humanity in an increasingly automated and interconnected world.

Believers and Sceptics: A Divided Legacy

Like many prophets before her, Baba Vanga's legacy is marked by both devotion and doubt. Her followers revere her as a true visionary, citing her many accurate predictions and her spiritual wisdom, while sceptics challenge the validity of her prophecies and question the methods she used to derive them. This tension between belief and skepticism is central to her place in history.

Followers and Devotees: Baba Vanga's prophecies inspired a devoted following, particularly in her home country of Bulgaria and throughout Eastern Europe. Her ability to provide personal guidance and predict global events made her a trusted figure for many who believed in her gift. For her followers, Baba Vanga was not just a prophet but a healer, counselor, and spiritual leader. Her predictions about natural disasters, political changes, and individual fates provided comfort and direction during times of uncertainty.

Criticism and Skepticism: Despite her widespread influence, Baba Vanga's prophecies have also been met with skepticism. Critics argue that many of her predictions were vague, open to interpretation, or applied retroactively to fit specific events. Others question whether her methods, which often relied on ritual and symbolism, can be considered reliable indicators of future events. This skepticism is part of a broader debate about the nature of prophecy itself—whether it is an expression of true clairvoyance or a reflection of human psychology and pattern-seeking behavior.

Cultural Impact: Regardless of belief or skepticism, Baba Vanga's influence on popular culture cannot be denied. Her name has become synonymous with prophecy, and her predictions are frequently cited in discussions about the future, particularly in media and online communities. Her prophecies have inspired books, documentaries, and even conspiracy theories, cementing her place as one of the most famous mystics of the modern era.

Baba Vanga and the Globalization of Prophecy

Baba Vanga's prophecies transcended national boundaries, gaining attention far beyond Bulgaria and the Balkans. Her global reach reflects the interconnected nature of the modern world, where ideas and information spread rapidly through media and technology. Her rise to international prominence demonstrates how prophecy, once a local or regional phenomenon, can now reach audiences across the globe.

International Fame: As word of Baba Vanga's predictions spread, she became a figure of global fascination. Her ability to predict major world events—such as the September 11 attacks, the 2004 tsunami, and the rise of certain political leaders—captured the imaginations of people from all walks of life. Her prophecies were translated into multiple languages, and she gained a following in countries as far away as Russia, the United States, and Japan.

THE ROLE OF MEDIA IN Shaping Her Legacy: Baba Vanga's rise to international prominence was largely facilitated by the media. Television programs, news articles, and online platforms helped disseminate her predictions to a global audience, often amplifying her reputation as a prophet. This media-driven spread of her prophecies reflects the role that modern communication technologies play in shaping the legacy of contemporary mystics and spiritual leaders.

Prophecy in a Globalized World: In an era defined by globalization, Baba Vanga's prophecies reflect the interconnectedness of humanity's future. Her predictions often addressed global issues—such as climate change, war, and technological disruption—affecting people across national and cultural boundaries. As the world becomes increasingly interdependent, Baba Vanga's vision of a shared future resonates with those seeking to understand the broader forces shaping human destiny.

Mysticism and the Human Desire for Certainty

Baba Vanga's enduring legacy is rooted in the human desire for certainty in an uncertain world. Throughout history, prophets and mystics have played a crucial role in providing guidance, comfort, and foresight during times of upheaval.

Baba Vanga's ability to address both personal and global concerns made her a figure of immense significance for those seeking answers about the future.

The Appeal of Prophecy: At the core of Baba Vanga's appeal is the universal human desire to know the future. In a world marked by unpredictability—whether due to political instability, environmental disasters, or personal crises—prophets like Baba Vanga offer a sense of control and understanding. Her ability to articulate visions of the future, even when shrouded in mystery or metaphor, gave people a framework for interpreting the unknown.

The Role of Mysticism in Modern Life: Baba Vanga's legacy speaks to the continued relevance of mysticism in the modern world. Despite the advances of science and technology, many people continue to seek spiritual insight and guidance from sources beyond the material world. Baba Vanga's predictions, while sometimes controversial, reflect this enduring human need to connect with something greater than ourselves—a force that offers meaning and purpose in the face of life's uncertainties.

A Bridge Between Worlds: For her followers, Baba Vanga was more than just a prophet; she was a bridge between the physical and spiritual worlds. Her ability to "see" beyond the ordinary senses made her a conduit for divine or cosmic knowledge, offering insights into both the immediate and distant future. This dual role as a seer and spiritual guide helped cement her status as one of the most influential mystics of the 20th century.

Baba Vanga's Legacy in Prophecy and Mysticism

As we look back on Baba Vanga's life and work, it becomes clear that her legacy extends far beyond the accuracy of her predictions. She represents the enduring power of prophecy in shaping how we understand the world and our place in it. Her ability to tap into a deeper, mystical realm of knowledge has left a lasting impact on both her followers and the broader cultural landscape.

A Symbol of Prophecy and Spiritual Insight: Baba Vanga's name has become synonymous with prophecy, and her predictions continue to inspire awe, curiosity, and debate. She stands as a symbol of humanity's quest for insight into the unknown, embodying the mystical traditions that have shaped cultures for centuries. Her ability to foresee global events, as well as her personal guidance to individuals, solidified her as one of the most influential seers of modern times.

Influence on Modern Mystics and Prophets: Baba Vanga's legacy has influenced a new generation of mystics and spiritual figures who draw upon her methods and predictions. She paved the way for contemporary prophets to engage with the global challenges of the 21st century, using their gifts to address issues such as climate change, technological advancement, and the future of humanity.

The Enduring Mystery of Baba Vanga: Even decades after her death, Baba Vanga remains a figure of mystery. Her methods of prophecy, her visions of the future, and her connection to spiritual forces continue to captivate believers and sceptics alike. Whether viewed as a true visionary or a product of cultural and psychological phenomena, Baba Vanga's place in history is secure—her legacy of mysticism and prophecy will continue to resonate for generations to come.

Conclusion: Baba Vanga's Place in the Pantheon of Prophets

Baba Vanga's prophecies, mysterious methods, and profound influence have cemented her place in the pantheon of prophets, alongside figures like Nostradamus, Edgar Cayce, and other visionary seers. Her predictions, while often cryptic and subject to interpretation, have shaped the way many view the future, offering both hope and caution.

In this chapter, we explored Baba Vanga's enduring legacy, from her role as a modern prophet to the global impact of her predictions. Her place in history is not merely as a predictor of events but as a symbol of the human desire to understand the mysteries of life and the future. Whether through her visions of global events or her spiritual counsel to individuals, Baba Vanga's work continues to inspire reflection on the power of prophecy and the importance of mystical insight in navigating the uncertainties of life.

As we look to the future, Baba Vanga's prophecies remind us that while the path ahead may be filled with challenges, the search for meaning, guidance, and understanding is a journey that transcends time and space—a legacy that endures beyond the boundaries of the physical world.

Don't miss out!

Visit the website below and you can sign up to receive emails whenever Andrew Parry publishes a new book. There's no charge and no obligation.

https://books2read.com/r/B-A-FROLC-YLKCF

BOOKS 2 READ

Connecting independent readers to independent writers.

About the Author

Andrew Parry is a dedicated researcher and author specializing in non-fiction works. His writing is driven by a deep passion for exploring the subjects that resonate with his core beliefs and concerns. Andrew's work reflects his profound commitment to addressing some of the most pressing issues facing humanity today, including the future of our species, the environment, and the looming threat of extinction.